Rethinking Language,
Mind, and Meaning

Rethinking Language, Mind, and Meaning

SCOTT SOAMES

PRINCETON UNIVERSITY PRESS
PRINCETON AND OXFORD

Published by Princeton University Press, 41 William Street,
Princeton, New Jersey 08540
In the United Kingdom: Princeton University Press, 6 Oxford Street,
Woodstock, Oxfordshire OX20 1TW

press.princeton.edu

Library of Congress Cataloging-in-Publication Data
Soames, Scott.
Rethinking language, mind, and meaning / Scott Soames.
pages cm.—(The Carl G. Hempel lecture series)
Includes bibliographical references and index.
ISBN 978-0-691-16045-0 (hardcover : alk. paper)
1. Thought and thinking. 2. Cognition. 3. Perception.
4. Meaning (Psychology) 5. Proposition (Logic) I. Title.
BF441.S635 2015
121'.68—dc23
2014023268

British Library Cataloging-in-Publication Data is available

This book has been composed in Charis SIL

Printed on acid-free paper. ∞

Printed in the United States of America

1 3 5 7 9 10 8 6 4 2

FOR

MARTHA, GREG, AND BRIAN

CONTENTS

ACKNOWLEDGMENTS

Thank you to the Philosophy Department of Princeton University for inviting me to give the Hempel Lectures in 2013 and to Princeton University Press for inviting me to do this book based on those lectures. Thanks also to all the friends, colleagues, and students who made my years at Princeton so rich, and to my wife Martha, who has made my post-Princeton years richer.

Rethinking Language, Mind, and Meaning

CHAPTER 1

The Need for New Foundations

In this book, I will argue that the revolution in the study of language, mind, and meaning led by advances in philosophical logic from Frege through Tarski, Kripke, Montague, and Kaplan must be reconceptualized. Although much progress has been made by adapting intensional logic to the study of natural language, the resulting theoretical framework has limitations that require rethinking much of what has guided us up to now. I will begin by sketching where we are in the study of linguistic meaning and how we got there, after which I will identify three main ways in which I believe the current theoretical framework must change.

The story begins with the development of symbolic logic by Gottlob Frege and Bertrand Russell at the end of the nineteenth and beginning of the twentieth centuries. Initially, their goal was to answer two questions in the philosophy of mathematics: *What is the source of mathematical knowledge?* and *What are numbers?* They answered (roughly) that *logic* is the source of mathematical knowledge, that *zero* is the set of concepts true of nothing, that *one* is the set of concepts true something, and only that thing, that *two* is the set of concepts true of some distinct x and y, and nothing else, and so on. Since the concept *being non-self-identical* is true of nothing, it is a member of zero; since the concept *being the Hempel lecturer in 2013* is true of me and only me, it is a member of the number one;

since the concept *being my son* is true of Greg and Brian Soames, and only them, it is a member of the number two. Other integers follow in train. Since numbers are sets of concepts, the successor of a number n is the set of concepts F such that for some x of which F is true, the concept *being an F which is not identical to x* is a member of n. Natural numbers are defined as those things that are members of every set that contains zero, and that, whenever it contains something, always contains its successor. Multiplication is defined as repeated addition, while addition is defined as repeated application of the successor function. In this way arithmetic was derived from what Frege and Russell took to be pure logic. When, in similar fashion, classical results of higher mathematics were derived from arithmetic, it was thought that all classical mathematics could be so generated. So, logic was seen the foundation of all mathematical knowledge.

That, at any rate, was the breathtaking dream of Frege and Russell. The reality was more complicated. Their first step was the development of the *predicate calculus* (of first and higher orders), which combined truth-functional logic, familiar from the Stoics onward, with a powerful new account of generality supplanting the more limited syllogistic logic dating back to Aristotle. The key move was to trade the subject/predicate distinction of syllogistic logic for an expanded version of the function/argument distinction from mathematics. Applied to quantification, this meant treating the claim *that something is F* as predicating *being true of something* of the property *being F* or, in Russell's convenient formulation, of the function that maps an object onto *the proposition that it is F*, while treating the claim *that everything is F* as predicating *being true of each object* of that property or function. The crucial point, resulting in a vast increase in expressive power, is the analysis of *all* and *some* as expressing higher-order properties of properties or propositional functions expressed by formulas of arbitrary complexity.[1]

Although the first-order fragment of Frege's system was sound and complete—in the sense of proving all and only genuine logical truths—the concepts needed to define and prove this (while also proving that the higher-order system was sound but, like all such systems, incomplete) were still fifty years away. In itself, this didn't defeat the reduction of mathematics to logic. More serious was the intertwining of this early stage of modern logic with what we now call "naïve set theory"—according to which for every stateable condition on objects there is a set (perhaps empty, perhaps not) of all and only the things satisfying it. To think of this as a principle of logic is to think that talk of something's *being so-and-so* is interchangeable with talk of its being in the set of so-and-so's.

When Russell's paradox demonstrated the contradiction at the heart of this system, it quickly became clear that the principles required to generate sets without falling into contradiction are less obvious, and open to greater doubt, than the arithmetical principles that Frege and Russell hoped to derive from them. This undercut the initial epistemological motivation for reducing mathematics to logic. Partly for this reason, the subsequent boundary that grew up between logic and set theory was one in which the latter came to be viewed as itself an elementary mathematical theory, rather than a part of logic. Reductions of mathematical theories to set theory could still be done, with illuminating results for the foundations of mathematics, but the philosophical payoff was not what Frege and Russell initially hoped for.[2]

---

[1] 'F' and 'G' are here used as schematic letters.

[2] This story is told in much greater detail in chapters 1, 2, 7, and 10 of Soames (2014b).

This *philosophical* shortcoming was compensated by the birth of new deductive disciplines—proof theory and model theory—to study the powerful new logical systems that had been developed. A modern system of logic consists of a formally defined language, plus a proof procedure, often in the form of a set of axioms and rules of inference. A proof is a finite sequence of lines each of which is an axiom or a formula obtainable from earlier lines by inference rules. Whether or not something counts as a proof is decidable merely by inspecting the formula on each line, and determining whether it is an axiom, and, if it isn't, whether it bears the structural relation to earlier lines required by the rules. Since these are trivially decidable questions, it can always be decided whether something counts as a proof, thus forestalling the need to prove that something is a proof. In a purely logical (first-order) system, the aim is to prove all and only the *logical truths,* and to be able to derive from any statement all and only its *logical consequences.*

These notions are defined *semantically.* To think of them in this way is to think of them as having something to do with *meaning.* Although this wasn't exactly how the founder of model theory, Alfred Tarski, initially conceived them, it is how his work was interpreted by Rudolf Carnap and many who followed. The key idea is that *we can study the meaning of sentences by studying what would make them true.* This is done by constructing abstract models of the world and checking to see which sentences are true in which models. When a sentence is true in all models it is a logical truth; when the truth of one sentence in a model always guarantees the truth of another, the second is a *logical consequence* of the first; when two sentences are always true together or false together they are *logically equivalent,* which is the logician's approximation of sameness of meaning.

By the mid-1930s, the model and proof theories of the first- and second-order predicate calculi were well understood and inspiring new projects. One was modal logic, which introduced an operator *it is logically/analytically/necessarily true that*—the prefixing of which to a standard logical truth produces a truth. Apart from confusion about what logical, semantic, or metaphysical notion was to be captured, the technical ideas soon emerged. Since the new operators are defined in terms of truth at *model-like elements*, logical models for modal languages had to contain such elements, now dubbed *possible world-states*, thought of as *ways the world could have been*. This development strengthened the Fregean idea that for a (declarative) sentence S to be meaningful is for S to represent the world as being a certain way, which is to impose conditions the world must satisfy if S is to be true.

Hence, it was thought, meaning could be studied by using the syntactic structure of sentences plus the representational contents of their parts to specify their truth conditions. With the advent of modality, these conditions were for the first time strong enough to approximate the *meanings of sentences*. To learn *what the world would have to be like* to conform to how a sentence (of a certain sort) represents it *is* to learn something approximating its meaning. The significance of this advance for the study of language can hardly be overstated. Having reached this stage, we had both a putative answer to the question *What is the meaning of a sentence?* and a systematic way of studying it.

This is roughly where the philosophically inspired study of linguistically encoded information stood in 1960. Since then, philosophers, philosophical logicians, and theoretical linguists have expanded the framework to cover large fragments of human languages. Their research program starts with the predicate calculi and is enriched piece by piece, as more natural-language constructions are added. Modal operators include *it is necessarily the case that, it could have been the case that,* and the counterfactual operator *if it had been*

the case that ___ , *then it would have been the case that* ___ . Operators involving time and tense can be treated along similar lines. Generalized quantifiers have been added, as have adverbs of quantification, and propositional attitude verbs such as *believe, expect,* and
know. We also have accounts of adverbial modifiers, comparatives,
intensional transitives, indexicals, and demonstratives. At each stage,
a language fragment for which we already have a truth-theoretic semantics is expanded to include more features found in natural language. As the research program advances, the fragments of which we
have a good truth-theoretic grasp become more powerful and more
fully natural language–like. Although there are legitimate doubts
about whether all aspects of natural language can be squeezed into
one or another version of this representational paradigm, the pros-
pects of extending the results so far achieved justify optimism about
eventually arriving at a time when vastly enriched descendants of the
original systems of Frege and Russell approach the expressive power
of natural language, allowing us to understand the most basic pro-
ductive principles by which information is linguistically encoded.

This, in a nutshell, is the dominant semantic conception in theoretical linguistics today. If all that remained were to fill in gaps and
flesh out empirical details, philosophers would have done most of
what was needed to transform their initial philosophical questions
about mathematics into scientific questions about language. However, we haven't yet reached that point. While the dominant conception has made progress in using truth conditions to *model* representational contents of sentences, it has not paid enough attention to
the demands that using and understanding language place on agents.
Given the logical, mathematical, and philosophical origins of the
enterprise, it could hardly have been otherwise. When what was at
stake was, primarily, the investigation of the logical, analytic, or
necessary consequences of mathematical and scientific statements,

there was no theoretically significant gap to be considered between what a sentence means and the claim it is used to make, and hence no need either to investigate how speaker-hearers might fill such gaps or to study what understanding and using a language consist in, and no need to individuate thoughts or meanings beyond necessary equivalence.

There have, to be sure, been important attempts to address these issues as the dominant semantic model has extended its reach beyond the formal languages of logic, mathematics, and science. We need, for example, to look no further than David Kaplan's *logic of demonstratives*, to find a way of accommodating the idea that what a sentence means and what it is standardly used to say are—though systematically related—not always the same. What we don't find in Kaplan, or in the dominant approach generally, is any retreat from the idea that advances in the understanding the semantics of natural language are closely and inextricably tied to advances in extending the reach of the methods of formal logic and model theory. This, I believe, must change if we are to reach our goal of founding a truly scientific study of language and information.

In this book, I will outline three steps in that direction. First, I will use examples involving several linguistic constructions to argue that we must stop oversimplifying the relationship between the information semantically encoded by (a use of) a sentence (in a context), on the one hand, and the assertions it is there used to make, the beliefs it is there used to express, and the information there conveyed by an utterance of it, on the other. It has often been assumed that the semantic content of a sentence is identical, or nearly so, with what one who accepts it thereby believes, and with what one who utters it thereby asserts. This is far too simple; there is a significant gap between the semantic contents of sentences and the information contents of their uses.

Second, I will argue that we need to pay more attention to what *understanding* a linguistic expression E requires—beyond, or other than, *knowing of* the representational content of E that it is the content of E. It is often assumed that since meaning is semantically encoded information, and since the information encoded by a nonindexical sentence S is the proposition p it expresses, understanding S is knowing of S that it encodes p. I will argue that this is not so. Semantic knowledge of this simple representational sort is insufficient for understanding because, as I will illustrate in chapter 4, to understand a word, phrase, or sentence is to be able to use it in expected ways in communicative interactions with members of one's linguistic community, which involves graded recognitional and inferential ability that often goes well beyond a cognitive grasp of content.[3] The semantic knowledge in question is also unnecessary for understanding a sentence because, as I will argue in chapters 2 and 4, to understand S is to be disposed to use S to entertain p—which, contrary to what is often assumed, doesn't require being disposed to make p the object of one's thought, or to predicate any relation holding between S and p. Once we have a proper understanding of what propositions really are, it will be easy to see that to entertain one is *not* to have any thought about or cognition of it at all, but to perform the cognitive operations in terms of which the proposition is defined.

This brings me to the final, and most foundational, change in the theoretical framework needed in our quest for a truly scientific study of language and information. Up to now, theorists have identified the semantic content of a sentence with information that represents the world as being a certain way, but they haven't yet given a plausible story about what such a piece of information is, whether

---

[3] This point is developed at length by my student Brian Bowman in his USC dissertation (2012).

linguistically encoded or not. This is our most urgent task, and the one on which I will concentrate most.

The currently dominant semantic approach correctly maintains that S represents things as being a certain way, and so has truth conditions, *because* the information S encodes—the proposition it expresses—represents things that way, and so has truth conditions. However, it misidentifies those propositions as functions from possible world-states to truth values, or, more simply, as sets of possible world-states (or other truth-supporting circumstances). However, neither such functions nor such sets can play the four roles typically demanded of propositions: (i) the primary bearers of truth and falsity, (ii) the objects of belief, assertion, and other attitudes, (iii) the contents of perceptual and cognitive states, and (iv) the meanings of (some) sentences. There are three main reasons that support this negative conclusion.

First, both functions from world-states to truth values and sets of such world-states are too coarse-grained to be meanings of sentences or objects of the attitudes. Worse, the strategies cooked up to mitigate the problem—(a) substituting finer-grained truth supporting circumstances for world-states, (b) developing a discourse model that substitutes so-called "diagonal propositions" for propositions semantically expressed as objects of crucial assertions, and (c) using two-dimensional semantic theories to assign pairs of coarse-grained propositions to sentences—have all failed to solve the problems they were supposed to address.[4]

Second, coarse-grainedness aside, neither sets of world-states nor functions from such to truth values can be meanings of sentences, while also being primary bearers of truth conditions. Meanings are

---

[4] Regarding (a), see Soames (1987, 2008); regarding (b), see Soames (2006c); regarding (c) see Soames (2005c).

the interpretations of sentences rather than entities that themselves require interpretation. But without interpretation by us, a set of world-states doesn't have truth conditions at all. In and of itself, such a set doesn't represent anything as being one way rather than another, and so doesn't impose any conditions the world must satisfy if the putative proposition is to be true. Consider the set containing just world-states 1, 2, and 3. Is it true or false? Since the set doesn't represent anything as being one way or another, it can't be either. We could, if we wanted, *interpret* it as representing *the actual world-state as being in the set,* and so as being true iff no world-state *outside* the set were the unique world-state that is instantiated. But we could equally well interpret it as representing the actual world-state as *not being in the set,* and so as being true iff no world-state *inside* it is instantiated. Without interpretation by us, the set doesn't represent anything, and doesn't have truth conditions. Since propositions aren't things we interpret, but are themselves the interpretations we give to sentences, they aren't sets of world-states.

The *function* that assigns *truth* to some world-states and *falsity* to others is no better. Suppose we replaced truth and falsity with 1 and 0. What does a function that assigns 1 to some states and 0 to others represent? Without interpretation by us, it doesn't represent anything. Nor, as indicated by (i)–(iv), does it help to appeal to truth and falsity rather than to 1 and 0.

(i)   Truth is the property that a proposition has when the world is as the proposition represents it to be, as well as a property which, when predicated of a proposition p, gives us a claim—*that p is true*—that one is warranted in accepting, asserting, rejecting, denying, believing, or doubting iff one is warranted in taking the same attitude to p. Since this is what truth is, propositions are conceptually prior to truth, in which case truth can't be one of the things from which propositions are constructed.

(ii) Even if this weren't so, the function that assigns world-states 1–3 truth, and all others falsity, doesn't, in and of itself, represent anything as being one way rather than another—any more than does the set of world-states of which it is the characteristic function. The illusion that it does comes from telling ourselves a story that relies on a different, conceptually prior, notion of propositions. In this story, which depends on thinking of world-states as properties that can be predicated of the universe, each assignment of a truth value to a world-state w is correlated with *the proposition that predicates w of the universe*—which is thereby true (false) iff the universe is (isn't) in state w. A function from world-states to truth values can then be associated with the (possibly infinite) disjunction of the propositions correlated with its assignments of truth to world-states. However, far from vindicating the idea that such functions *are* propositions, it presupposes an antecedent conception of propositions according to which they are *not* such functions.

(iii) The conception of propositions as functions from world-states to truth values goes hand in hand with a conception of properties as functions from world-states to extensions. This flies in the face of taking the "worlds" of possible-worlds semantics to be properties—for surely a world-state *isn't* a function from world-states to anything. But if properties have to be taken as basic, rather than explained away, surely propositions should have the same status.

(iv) It is better *not* to take world-states as primitive either. The best account takes them to be properties of making complete world-stories (the constituents of which are propositions) true. Thus, *both truth and world-states* are conceptually downstream from propositions, and so are not the conceptual building blocks from which propositions are constructed.[5]

Finally, the proponent of possible-worlds semantics faces a dilemma. Suppose, as is common, the theorist takes the two-place predicate x_S *is true at* y_W (where the variable 'x_S' is assigned a sentence S and the variable 'y_W' is assigned a world-state W) to be an undefined primitive. Then, the theorist has no way of answering the question, "What, if anything, does the theorem *For all world-states* y_W, *'Mi libro es rojo' is true at* y_W *iff at* y_W, *my book is red,* tell us about the meaning of the Spanish sentence?" By contrast, suppose one understands x_S *is true at* y_W (relative to an assignment of S and W to the respective variables) as telling us that if W were instantiated then *the proposition that S actually expresses* would be true. To understand 'is true at' in this way is to presuppose antecedent notions of *the proposition S expresses* and *the monadic notion of truth* applying to it. Taking these antecedent notions at face value, the theorist can use the commonsense truism—⌈if 'S' means, or is used to express, the proposition that P, then necessarily the proposition expressed by 'S' is true iff P⌉—together with the truth-conditional theorem—*For all world-states* y_W, *'Mi libro es rojo' is true at* y_W *iff at* y_W, *my book is red*—to conclude that the sentence 'Mi libro es rojo' means (expresses) something necessarily equivalent to the proposition that my book is red.

Although taking this route doesn't identify what the sentence means, it does allow us to extract substantial information about its meaning from a statement of its truth conditions at possible world-states. The price of this happy result is the obligation to explicate the *prior notions* of *the proposition expressed by S* and *the monadic notion of truth* applying to it. Since possible-worlds semanticists have typically refused to acknowledge this price, let alone to pay it, they are in no

---

[5] See Soames (2007a) and chapter 5 of (2010a).

THE NEED FOR NEW FOUNDATIONS

position to claim that their theories provide any information at all about meaning. By contrast, those of us who wish to preserve the great progress in the study of language made by applying the methods of intensional semantics to natural language must find a way of paying the price for them by explaining what propositions really are and how they can be added to possible-worlds semantic theories as genuine truth-condition determiners. This is our most serious problem.

It is tempting to think that it can be solved by returning to traditional Fregean or Russellian conceptions of structured propositions. However, the utility of such conceptions is severely limited. Taking their cues from these traditional theories, many contemporary proponents of structured propositions address the coarse-grainedness problem by using n-tuples of objects and properties to model propositions. Although this approach does a better job of individuating the objects of the attitudes than does any conception of propositions as constructions of truth-supporting circumstances, contemporary conceptions of structured propositions don't go far enough. As I will argue at length in later chapters, they, like possible-worlds conceptions of propositions, wrongly foreclose needed analyses of the assertions made, and beliefs expressed, by many utterances, including, most obviously, utterances of propositional attitude ascriptions. Worse, the n-tuples standardly employed by contemporary proponents of structured propositions are merely models of the real things. Since n-tuples, or any other purely formal structures of objects and properties, don't, without interpretation by us, represent the world as being one way rather than another, they can't be meanings or primary bearers of truth conditions. The same is true of the propositions originally proposed by Frege and Russell, as attested by recent work on the so-called *problem of the unity of the proposition*, which undermined them.[6]

---

[6] See Soames (2010c); Soames (2014b), chapters 2, 3, 7, and 9; and King, Soames, and Speaks (2014), chapter 3.

The concern underlying the so-called unity problem was also the basis for Donald Davidson's most telling objection to semantic theories that postulated structured propositions as meanings of sentences. Commenting on traditional conceptions of propositions in 1967, he aptly remarked:

> Paradoxically, the one thing meanings do not seem to do is oil the wheels of a theory of meaning—at least as long as we require of such a theory that it non-trivially give the meaning of every sentence in the language. My objection to meanings in the theory of meaning is not that they are abstract or that their identity conditions are obscure, but that they have no demonstrated use.[7]

His complaint was that taking structured propositions to be the meanings (or, in more recent terminology, *semantic contents*) of sentences (relative to contexts) doesn't help in constructing a theory of meaning, unless one can read off how a sentence represents things to be from the specification of the structured proposition it expresses. Since this crucial information *can't* be read off Fregean, Russellian, or any other traditional account of structured propositions, a new conception of propositions is needed.[8]

To provide such a conception, while retaining the insights of Frege and Russell, we must reverse their explanatory priorities. Instead of deriving the intentionality of agents from independently representational propositions, we must explain the intentionality of propositions in terms of the conceptually prior ability of agents to represent the world in thought and perception. This will be my task in the next chapter.

---

[7] Davidson (2001), quoted at pp. 21–22.
[8] See Soames (2010c), pp. 49–55, for discussion.

The Metaphysics and Epistemology of Information

WHAT ARE PROPOSITIONS?

In this chapter I sketch a theory of propositions capable of playing the roles required of them in our theories of thought, language, and perception. The key constraint shaping the account is that real propositions are *not* things we, or other cognitive agents, *interpret*; they are *not instruments* we or they *use* to carry information; they are *not* entities we or they *endow* with intentionality. Rather, *propositions are inherently representational entities that are capable of being true or false, independent of any actual use to which we or other agents put them.* The constraint is demanding, since, as I indicated in the previous chapter, there are reasons to believe that no set-theoretic construction of objects, properties, world-states, or other denizens of Plato's heaven could ever be inherently representational bearers of truth conditions in this sense.

The most fundamental defect of traditional conceptions of propositions is that the intentionality of propositions is treated as conceptually and explanatorily prior to that of agents who bear attitudes to them. On the traditional conception, agents who entertain propositions cognitively represent things as bearing certain properties and standing in certain relations *because* the propositions they entertain do. The problem with trying to derive the intentionality of agents from the unexplained intentionality of propositions is that we have no understanding of what such primitively representational entities are, of how we cognize them, or of why our cognizing them in the required way results in *our ability* to represent things as bearing properties and standing in relations. Suppose, however, we start at the other end, taking it as an uncontested certainty that *agents* represent things as being certain ways when they think of them as being those ways. We then ask, *"What kind of entity P and what relation R can play the role of propositions and entertaining, by virtue of the fact that for an agent to bear R to an entity of kind P guarantees that the agent represents things as being a certain way?"* If we can find such a P and R, we might explain the intentionality of entities of kind P by deriving it from the intentionality of agents who bear R to them. For example, we may identify a particular entity of kind P such that for an agent to bear R to it *just is* for the agent to represent object o as *being red.* Such an entity might then be deemed true iff that way of representing o represents o as it really is. The entity itself—the putative proposition—could then be counted as representing o as red in a secondary, derivative sense. For it to represent o in this sense is simply for any arbitrary agent who entertains it to represent o as being red in the primary sense (of representing something to be so-and-so).

When the task of identifying propositions is thought of in this way, one answer to the question "What are propositions and what is it to entertain one?" stands out above all others. *Propositions are repeatable, purely representational, cognitive acts or operations the performance of which results in concrete cognitive events; to entertain a proposition is to perform it.* Suppose, for example, that I perceive or think of a certain book B as red. In such a case, I *do* something, namely, perform the act of predicating *redness* of B, which is to *represent B as red.* The sense in which *the act* can be said to represent B as red is analogous to the derivative sense in which some acts are said to be intelligent, stupid, or thoughtful. For *an act* to be intelligent is *not* for it to be a quick and powerful thinker, even though that is what it is for an agent to be intelligent (in the primary sense). By the same token, for an act to be stupid is *not* for it to be a slow learner; and for an act to be thoughtful is *not* for it to be empathetic. For an act to be one of these *is* for it to be one the performance of which marks an agent as behaving intelligently, stupidly, or thoughtfully—which is how those who are intelligent, stupid, or thoughtful often act.

The related sense in which for an act to have a certain property is for an agent who performs it to have a related property is also exhibited by insults and irresponsible actions. For example, we say that an act is insulting when for one to perform it is for one to insult someone; we say that it is irresponsible when to perform it is to neglect one's responsibilities. In saying this, we are not saying that the act type itself does anything to cause offense or that it has been remiss in fulfilling its obligations. Since an act neither *does* anything in the sense an agent does, nor has any responsibilities, the sense in which an act may be insulting or irresponsible is not the same as the sense in which an agent who performs it insults or is irresponsible. When one says, referring to an act, "That was an irresponsible thing to do," what one says is true iff it is possible to accurately describe the agent as doing something—e.g., as making a promise with no intention of keeping it in such-and-such circumstances—from which it follows that the agent acts irresponsibly. Taking act types to be fine-grained—in the sense in which traveling to work is distinct from driving there (because to perform the latter is also to perform the former but not conversely)—we may characterize irresponsible acts as those every possible performance of which involves neglecting one's responsibilities. The point is not that this kind of smooth transition between properties of agents and related properties of acts *always* occurs; it most certainly doesn't. However, it can and often does occur when the connection between the two properties is particularly tight and there is reason to exploit it.

The connection between the secondary sense in which representational acts represent and the primary sense in which the agents who perform them do is a case in point. In addition to assessing an agent's habitual or overall accuracy in representing his or her environment, we also need to assess the accuracy of the agent's sayings or cognitions, one by one. For this, we need truth and falsity, plus cognitive doings that *represent* things as being various ways, *where the sense in which they represent things is simply that performing them guarantees that agents represent those things.* When to perceive or think of o as P is to represent o as it is, we identify an entity—a particular sort of perceiving or thinking—plus a property that entity has when this sort of perceiving or thinking is accurate. The entity is a proposition, which is the cognitive act of representing o as P. The property is truth, which the act has iff to perform it is for one to represent o as o really is.

To *entertain* a proposition is *not*, as Frege or the early Russell would have you believe, to think of it in a special way; it is to perform it. This is the attitude on which other propositional attitudes are based. To *judge* that B is red is perform the predication in an affirmative manner, which involves accepting it as a basis for possible action. To affirm or accept that B is red is not to predicate any property of the act, or to make *it* an object of cognition, but for one's performance of it to involve forming, or activating already formed, dispositions to act, both cognitively and behaviorally, toward B in ways conditioned by one's attitudes toward red things. In short, to *judge* that B is red is for one's predicating redness of B to involve one's forming or activating certain dispositions. To *believe that B is red* is (very roughly) to be disposed to judge that it is. To *know* that B is red is, roughly, for B to be red, to believe that B is red, and to be safe, or to be cognitively justified, in so believing. To *assert* that B is red is to commit oneself, by uttering something, to knowing that B is red.

These attitudes—judgment, belief, knowledge, and assertion—all aim at truth. But the story is the same for other attitudes—e.g., doubting, denying, disproving, and imagining—that don't aim at truth. Nevertheless, the objects of these attitudes—the things doubted, denied, disproved, or imagined—may be true or false, just as the things judged, believed, known, or asserted may be. Indeed, the very same proposition (e.g., *that B is red*) that is believed by one person may be doubted, denied, disproved, or merely considered by another. This suggests that the intentionality of both sets of attitudes—in the sense of being about certain things, which they represent in certain ways—is due to something common to them all and more basic than each. Thus, it is not any of these *attitudes* but their objects that, in the first instance, represent things as being certain ways, and so have truth conditions independently of agents' further affirmative, negative, or noncommittal stances toward them.

Faced with this fact, one may wonder how, if propositions have their truth conditions independently of *all attitudes* agents bear to them, the intentionality of agents can be the source of the intentionality of propositions. Although it is natural to be puzzled, the premise of the question is incorrect.[1] If the intentionality of propositions *were* independent of *all* attitudes agents bore to them, the intentionality of agents *wouldn't* be the source of the intentionality of propositions. But the intentionality of propositions *isn't* independent of the intentionality of *all* attitudes. The intentionality of a proposition p *just is* the intentionality of the conceptually fundamental ur-attitude of *entertaining* p. To entertain the proposition that B is red *is* to represent B as red. The obvious intentionality of this act *is* the

---

[1] Thanks to Paul Boghossian for raising this issue.

intentionality of the proposition because the act of entertaining the proposition *just is* the proposition. After all, the act of performing any act A is identical with A. Since entertaining a proposition is performing it, the intentionality of the act of entertaining it is the intentionality of the proposition itself.

This, I propose, is the basis of a plausible naturalistic epistemology and metaphysics of propositions. Since entertaining, believing, and knowing p don't require cognizing p, any organism that can perceive or think of things in its environment as being certain ways can bear these attitudes to propositions *whether or not it can predicate properties of propositions, or know anything about them.* Knowing or believing something *about* propositions requires a further cognitive ability that human beings have, but that some less sophisticated cognitive agents don't: the ability to focus on one's own cognitive acts and distinguish them from one another. One who can do this can, in principle, ascribe propositional attitudes to oneself and others, and predicate properties of propositions. Focusing on their own cognitive experience, sophisticated agents can discriminate different propositions as different particular ways of thinking or perceiving. This, in turn, allows them to acquire the notion of truth, in part from numerous examples—"the proposition *that o is red* is true if o is red, it isn't true if o isn't red," etc.—and in part by recognizing the general point that a proposition is true iff things are as it represents them to be. In this way, the cognitive conception of propositions avoids the obscure Platonic epistemology of traditional conceptions and demystifies our acquaintance with, and knowledge of, propositions by taking both to be grounded in concrete cognitive experience.

That is the idea behind propositions as purely representational cognitive acts or operations, or sequences of such. In the simplest case, the act is predicating a property of an object. More complex propositions are more complex acts or sequences, but the idea is the same. In speaking of predications and other cognitive operations as *acts,* I *don't* mean that they are always intentional (as opposed to unintentional) or even conscious. They aren't. Nevertheless, they are *doings* in which things are cognized as being one way or another. The result is representation. What a proposition represents is *always* read off the sequence of cognitive acts with which it is identified. The truth conditions of a proposition are derived from a statement of what it represents. Thus, a proposition that represents o as being red (without representing anything further) is true iff o is red. Truth conditions are relativized to world-states by characterizing a proposition p as being true at w iff *were w instantiated, and hence actual, things would be as p (always) represents them to be. What p represents* is *not* indexed to world-states; *p represents what any agent who entertains p (at any conceivable world-state) represents by performing p.* Since this doesn't vary from world-state to world-state, the truth conditions of a proposition don't vary from state to state. So, *the proposition that o is red* is true at w iff were w instantiated, o would be as any conceivable agent who entertains it (at any epistemically possible world-state) would thereby represent o as being. It follows that no one has to entertain *the proposition that o is red*, or any other proposition, at w in order for it to be true at w.

Since propositions are cognitive acts, one may think that in order for any cognitive acts to exist at w, some agents must perform some cognitive acts at w.[2] Fortunately, whether or not this is so is not much of an issue. Suppose it is so. From this supposition plus the previous result it follows that propositions can be true at

---

[2] It would, I think, be too much to require an act to have been performed in order for it to exist. When acts are complex and performing them requires performing a series of basic constituent acts—like identifying a property and an object and predicating the former of the latter—it may be enough that each of the constituent acts have been performed. For a discussion of this, see my chapters 6 and 12 of King, Soames, and Speaks (2014). Here, I confine myself to the natural thought that in order for any acts to exist at w some agents must perform some act or other at w.

world-states without existing there. But this is no cause for puzzlement. If p represents x as F, then for p to be true at w is just for x to be F at w. Since this carries no expectation that the proposition exists at w, its existence or nonexistence is irrelevant to its truth. It might, of course, be argued that in order for a proposition to represent at all, it must be epistemically possible for some possible agent or other to entertain, i.e., perform, it. This in turn might be seen as requiring the proposition to exist at some epistemically possible world-state. Suppose that it does. This has no effect on the unproblematic result that propositions can be true at world-states at which they don't exist. Given what propositions are, we don't need any portentous *true-in* a world-state vs. *true-at* a world-state distinction to ensure their truth at world-states at which they don't exist.

One might, however, wonder what it is to predicate a property of an object. Though I don't have a definition, there are some things to be said. To predicate redness of B is to perceptually or cognitively represent B as red, which is to see, visualize, imagine, or cognize B as red in some other way. These are different *ways* of predicating, *not different doings in addition to predicating.* Seeing B as red is *not* predicating redness of B *plus doing something else* (the doing of which is no part of the predicating), nor is imagining B as red predicating redness *plus doing a different something else.* To see B as red is to predicate redness of it *in a certain way*; to imagine B as red is to predicate redness of it *in a different way.* Since these different *ways* don't involve performing a second act the doing of which is no part of the predicating, there is no bare event of predicating redness of o that isn't identical with one of seeing o as red, visualizing o as red, imagining o as red, or cognizing o as red *in some other way.* There are no mode-neutral events of bare predication.

We also predicate redness of B when we judge or assert that B is red. Whether or not doing these things involves doing something distinct from and independent of predicating redness of B, as opposed merely to predicating redness of B in a distinctive way, is less clear than one might think. To judge B to be red is to predicate redness of B *affirming what one has done*, which is to predicate redness of B in a way that involves forming or activating certain distinctive cognitive and behavioral dispositions. Is this to *do* something else, over and above predicating—in the sense in which sending a signal by raising first one's left, and then one's right, arm involves performing two separate and independent acts? Or is it simply to predicate redness of B in its own special (affirmative) way—in the sense in which driving to work is simply traveling to work in a special way? Although I incline to the latter, I am not sure how much it matters what we say about this question. Either way, all *events* of judging o to be red involve a positive commitment to the redness of B.[3]

Asserting that B is red by uttering "B is red" is more complicated. Here the predication involves the sub-acts (i) using the word 'red' to identify the property predicated, (ii) using the name 'B' to identify the target of predication, and (iii) using the phrase 'is red' to predicate the identified property of the identified object. We may compare this complex act *CP* of predication to the simple predicative act *SP* of (i) identifying (no matter how) the property *redness* to be predicated, (ii) identifying (no matter how) the predication target B, and (iii) predicating the identified property of the identified target. *SP* is just like *CP* except that it abstracts away from whatever different sub-acts may be employed to identify the property predicated and its predication target. Thus, its relation to *CP* is rather like the relation between the act of traveling to work and the act of driving to work. In both cases although anyone who performs the latter also performs the former, one may perform the former without performing the latter. Next consider an assertive instance of *CP* in which the agent performs the

---

[3] Similar issues arise with *doubting that B is red*, even though here there is no positive commitment to B's being red.

act *AP* of asserting that B is red. Does performing *AP* involve performing *CP* plus some further independent act, or is *AP* simply a special
assertive way of performing the linguistic predication *CP*? Again, I
incline to the latter alternative, without insisting on it.

The key point here is the significance of the distinction between
SP and *CP*. Since the two purely cognitive acts predicate the same
property of the same thing, they are representationally identical but
cognitively distinct. The fact that both are propositions turns out to
have important and far-reaching consequences, which I will discuss
in chapter 4. Here, I simply note that, due to the public nature of
language and the ability of its speakers to avail themselves of contents with which they are not otherwise familiar, those who have
never encountered either B or redness are able to predicate the latter
of the former.

Abstracting away from any of the different cognitive means of
identifying the property predicated and the target of which it is
predicated, we have seen that there is a single proposition, *SP*, distinct from all others, which consists simply of predicating redness B.
Subject to qualifications, we may further suppose that there is a
single proposition *semantically encoded* by the sentence 'B is red'. But
cognitive events in which one *entertains* that proposition may be
events in which one entertains other propositions too. This is always
so when an agent entertains *SP* by virtue of entertaining *CP*, or by
entertaining any other proposition that is distinguished from *SP*
solely by sub-acts involving items, like linguistic expressions, used
to identify the property predicated or its predication target. However, it also happens in other ways as well. When we see or visualize
B as red, we also see or visualize it as some specific shade, as well as
having other properties. Similarly, when we imagine or think of B as
red, there is often something other than being red that goes into our
cognition of the predication target. In such cases we predicate

redness plus other properties of B, thereby entertaining several propositions. Predicating properties often comes in clusters, as do entertaining, judging, believing, and asserting propositions.

Although propositions are the objects of assertion and primary bearers of truth, we also speak of sentences, or sentences in contexts, as being true. A proper semantic theory captures this by first assigning objects, properties, functions, and operations to words and phrases. Sentences are assigned propositions, which are sequences of cognitive acts involving these things, specified in a way that allows us to read off how these propositional acts represent things. A proposition p is true at a world-state w iff were w to be instantiated things would be as p represents them. Sentences (in contexts) may be said to bear the truth conditions of the propositions they semantically express. However, this special notion of truth conditions must not be confused with a different, more ordinary, sense in which uses of sentences have truth conditions. Typically when we speak of the truth or falsity of a sentence as used on a given occasion, we mean the truth or falsity of the proposition or propositions it is used on that occasion to *assert*—which may go beyond, or even fail to include, the proposition semantically expressed by the sentence uttered.

Before illustrating how cognitive propositions can be integrated into semantic theories, and the advantages of doing so, I pause to flag an objection. *Propositions, the objection maintains, can't be acts because propositions aren't things we do! We can entertain the proposition that arithmetic is incomplete but we can't do it; to think otherwise is to make a category mistake.* I disagree; to think otherwise is to realize that our task is not to capture so-called "intuitions" about our untutored thought and talk, but to articulate a conception of propositions capable of playing the roles required of them in our philosophical, and fledgling scientific, theories of language and mind.

Because of this, ordinary-language arguments about what propositions cannot be aren't decisive.

Nor are such arguments normally taken to be decisive in semantics or the philosophy of language. Quite apart from foundational
metaphysical questions about what propositions are, it is common in
these fields to take them to be the meanings—or *semantic contents*—of some nonindexical sentences, despite the fact that this cuts
directly against the grain of some ordinary ways of speaking about
meaning. How much this identification cuts against the grain is illustrated by the following passage from Richard Cartwright (1962).

> If what someone asserts on some occasion [namely a proposi-
> tion] is itself the meaning which the words he utters have, on
> that occasion of their utterance, then anything predicable of
> what he asserts must also be predicable of the meaning of his
> words. But it is obvious on very little reflection that ever so
> many things predicable of what is asserted cannot (on pain of
> nonsense) be predicated of the meaning of a sentence. And the
> fundamental point to be noticed in this connection is that al-
> though we may predicate of something asserted that it is (or
> was) asserted, this cannot be predicated of the meaning of a
> sentence. *It simply makes no sense to say that someone asserted
> the meaning of a sentence* . . . . Just as the meanings of sentences
> cannot be asserted, neither can they be affirmed, denied, con-
> tradicted, questioned, challenged, discounted, confirmed, sup-
> ported, verified, withdrawn, repudiated, and whereas what is
> asserted can be said to be accurate, exaggerated, unfounded,
> overdrawn, probable, improbable, plausible, true, or false,
> none of these can be said of the meaning of a sentence.[4]

---

[4] At pp. 49–50 of the 1986 reprinting, my emphasis.

To appreciate Cartwright's point it is enough to consider examples like (1a) and (1b).

    1a. Bill asserted/proved/contradicted/supported/questioned/ withdrew the proposition that mathematics is reducible to logic.

    1b. *Bill asserted/proved/contradicted/supported/questioned/ withdrew the meaning of the sentence 'Mathematics is reducible to logic'.

Whereas the examples in (1a) sound fine, those in (1b) sound like category mistakes—i.e., to be incoherent or without sense (when they are not taken as suggesting some entirely different content). A similar distinction is illustrated by (2a) and (2b).

    2a. The proposition that mathematics is reducible to logic is plausible/probable/untrue.

    2b. *The meaning of the sentence 'Mathematics is reducible to logic' is plausible/probable/untrue.

But, in fact, the examples in (1b) and (2b) are *not* incoherent or without sense, as Cartwright himself later came to realize.[5] Given this, we need not deny that propositions can be meanings (in at least some reasonable sense of 'meanings') even though certain things truly attributable to propositions initially sound as if they couldn't be true of meanings, and conversely.[6]

A similar point can be made about the identification of propositions with purely representational cognitive acts. We do, of course,

---

[5] See the argument in the addenda, written in 1986, on pp. 52–53.

[6] One of the themes of this work—to be developed further in the last section of this chapter and in chapters 4 and 11—is that our pretheoretic notion of linguistic meaning, which is closely tied to understanding, contains at least two dimensions that need to be pulled apart. In speaking of propositions as the meanings of some sentences, I have in mind one of these two dimensions.

have lots of particular thoughts about propositions, the relations they bear to one another, and the sentences that express them. However, our general pretheoretic conception of what they are isn't very substantial. Insofar as we have one—apart being from the bearers of truth and objects of the attitudes—it is, I should think, that they are ways of thinking of, or mentally representing, things. It is this to which we philosophers appeal when we explain propositions to students or other nonphilosophers using truisms like *When we believe or assert something, there is something we believe or assert.* When we then ask *What are these things?*, the typical unprompted response is that they are "ways of thinking, conceiving, or imagining things"—cognitive acts, operations, episodes, or states in which agents think, imagine, conceive, or represent things as being certain ways. Because this is such a natural thought, the neophyte thinks that when the things thought of, imagined, conceived, or represented are as they are thought, imagined, conceived, or represented to be, the thought/proposition is true.

The result of this probing of common sense is in keeping with the conception of propositions as purely representational cognitive acts. The problem, of course, is that in making propositions things agents do, this conception also has a highly counterintuitive consequence. The difficulty we face is, as Cartwright's prescient article was designed to show, that every other articulated conception of what propositions are has counterintuitive consequences of its own. Since we need propositions in our theories, we shouldn't be satisfied with continuing to regard them as mysterious we-know-not-whats. Instead, we need to articulate informative theoretical conceptions of what propositions are, to explore their theoretical advantages, and to weigh those against their pretheoretic costs.

That will be my strategy. In the remainder of this chapter and those that immediately follow, I will spell out the advantages to be gained from adopting an act-based conception of propositions. With those advantages in mind, I will return in the penultimate chapter to the foundational metaphysics and epistemology of propositions. There, I will summarize the case for identifying propositions with purely representational cognitive acts, identify the source of the erroneous "intuition" that propositions can't be things we do, and indicate how we are able to arrive at knowledge of propositions without knowing—and even while harboring misleading "intuitions" about—what they are. The final chapter will be devoted to suggesting strategies for tackling remaining unanswered questions. Until those two chapters, I will be engaged in constructing the positive theory.

SEMANTICS: COMPLEX SENTENCES
AND PROPOSITIONS

I start with simple sentences involving direct reference and predication. For each name we specify a referent and for each simple predicate an n-place property. Example (3) is an interesting case.

3. The proposition expressed by 'Socrates exists' is the cognitive act of predicating existence of Socrates, which represents him as existing.

Socrates's nonexistence doesn't prevent us from referring to, or predicating properties of, him. Since the proposition that he exists is the act of predicating existence of him, it obviously exists, even though he doesn't exist. The idea that the existence of a structured proposition requires the existence of its constituents is the result of the wrong conception of propositions.

Next we add operators mapping properties onto properties—negation and disjunction, for example. When predicating one property represents x as *being A* and predicating another represents x as *being B*, predicating the negation of the first represents x as *not being*

A, while predicating the disjunction of the two represents x as *being A or B*. Similarly, for conjunction. This gives us the examples (4).

4a. The proposition expressed by 'Fido isn't human' is the act of negating *being human*, and predicating *not being human* of Fido. This proposition represents Fido as not being human.

4b. The proposition expressed by 'Martin is fat and happy' is the act of conjoining *being fat* and *being happy*, and predicating *being fat and happy* of Martin. This proposition represents Martin as being fat and happy.

4c. The proposition expressed by 'Mary isn't fat or happy' is the act of disjoining *being fat* and *being happy*, negating *being fat or happy*, and predicating *not being fat or happy* of Mary. This proposition represents Mary as not being fat or happy.

Examples like (4d) in which the truth predicate is negated are of special interest. When S is a declarative sentence, the clause ⌈that S⌉ is a directly referential term designating the proposition expressed by S. This gives us results like (4d).

4d. The proposition expressed by 'That Los Angeles is west of San Francisco isn't true' is the act that consists of (i) negating *being true*, (ii) identifying the predication target of the resulting property, *not being true*, by entertaining the proposition that Los Angeles is west of San Francisco (i.e., by predicating *being west* of ‹Los Angeles, San Francisco›), and (iii) predicating *not being true* of the proposition so identified. This proposition represents the proposition that Los Angeles is west of San Francisco as not being true.

This way of negating propositions requires making them *objects of predication*. Since the ability to entertain p *doesn't* guarantee one can think thoughts *about* p, not all agents capable of bearing attitudes to propositions can predicate properties of them. If one can't do this, one can't predicate untruth of propositions. However, it is plausible that even unsophisticated agents can negate propositions. If they can, it would seem that there should be another way of negating them—and of conjoining and disjoining them too.

It would appear that there is. Let p represent *A as being F* (and nothing more) and let q represent *B as being G* (and nothing more). To *disjoin* p and q is to entertain p, to entertain q, and to operate on p and q so as to represent *A as being F or B as being G*. Similarly for conjoining and negating propositions, which, like disjunction, are *operations* on propositions that don't involve predicating anything of them. On this picture, in which to negate p is to represent *Not A's being F*, all propositions involve predications at some level, but some propositions are operations on constituents that are, or depend on, predications. With this, we get truth-functional cognition without making propositions objects of thought.

But there is a worry. In order for there to be truth-conditional representation, something, or some things, must be represented as being some way. It is not obvious what is so represented when a negation represents *Not A's being F*, or when a disjunctive proposition represents *A as being F or B as being G*. The kind of representation that is needed is not the kind in which a particular dot on a map represents Los Angeles (which doesn't endow the representing entity with truth conditions). For truth conditions to come into play, something must be represented as being some way. So, we must ask, *What is represented as being what way by the act that represents Not A's being F, or by the act that represents A as being F or B as being G?* The easy thought is that it is *the world, the universe,* or *reality* that is represented as *not being such that A is F* or as *being such that A is F or B is G*. But that may seem extravagant. If the goal was to make truth-functional cognition safe for agents with cognitive powers too limited to predicate properties of propositions, it is not evident that the goal can be achieved by requiring them to represent *the universe* as being a certain way.[7]

With negation, it would be enough if the cognitive agent in question represented its immediate environment E as *not being such that A is F*. Then, for E to be as it is represented would be for E not to be such that A is F, which is simply for it *not to be that A is F*. In fact, the agent could be seen as representing any object we like, including A, as *not being such that A is F*. With this we are led to a promising thought. We may characterize the agent as indiscriminately representing *everything*—i.e., each thing—as not being such that A is F—by virtue of its being a matter of indifference which particular things are so represented (since either everything will be as represented or nothing will). The agent might even be viewed as *predicating* the unusual property *not being such that A is F*, identifying its predication targets as any and all objects arbitrarily.[8] With this, we arrive at an appropriately deflationary understanding of what it is to represent *the world* as not being such that A is F—deflationary because it doesn't require one to have a conception of *any single thing* as somehow being *the totality of all things*. Understanding the negation operation in this way, we can read off what the negation of p represents, and hence what its truth conditions are, provided that we are given what p represents. The same point holds for conjunctions and disjunctions. In this way, we can make sense of truth-functional cognition without predicating properties of propositions.

Conjunctions and disjunctions are useful in illustrating further points about the ways in which propositions are representational. Although I maintain that all propositions are purely representational

---

[7] Thanks to Stephen Schiffer for pressing this worry.

[8] The manner in which properties like this can be generated from already existing cognitive propositions is explaining of Soames (2014d), pp. 226–27.

acts, I do not maintain the converse. Suppose, as some may think, that "conjunctive acts" and "disjunctive acts" are themselves acts, in the sense that when a and b are acts, *doing both* and *doing either* are further acts. Then, some may maintain, the fact that *predicating redness of o* and *predicating greenness of o** are purely representational cognitive acts guarantees that the "conjunctive act" *predicating redness of o and predicating greenness of o** and the "disjunctive act" *predicating redness of o or predicating greenness of o** are themselves purely representational cognitive acts. But even if they are, they are not propositions, because they are not representational in the right way.

First consider the "disjunctive act." For an act to be a proposition, every possible performance of it must be one in which the agent represents one and the same thing (or things) as being one and the same way (or ways). The "act" of *either predicating redness of o or predicating greenness of o** doesn't satisfy this condition, since some performances of it represent only o as being red and some represent only o* as being green. Hence the act itself is not a proposition.

The contrast between the "conjunctive act" *predicating redness of o and predicating greenness of o** and the act of entertaining a conjunction illustrates a related point. Truth-functionally compound *propositions* are complex representational acts involving sub-acts that are themselves propositional. One who performs these complex acts performs their constituent sub-acts in order to obtain arguments for further cognitive operations that result, ultimately, in arriving at one's final destination. Consider one who negates the proposition *that o is red and o* is green.* One who does this predicates redness of o and greenness of o* (thereby entertaining the propositions *that o is red* and *that o* is green*) with the intention of applying the *conjoining* operation to the propositions entertained. The agent applies this operation to those propositions with the further intention of applying the negation operation to the entertained proposition *that o is red and o* is green.*

With this in mind, note the relationship between the compound representational act that is identical with the conjunctive proposition and the "conjunctive act" *predicating redness of o and predicating greenness of o**. Anyone who performs the former performs the latter, but not conversely. To perform the latter it is necessary not simply to represent *o as being red* and to represent *o* as being green*, but also to represent *o as being red and o* as being green* (thereby representing each thing as being such that o is red and o* is green). One who merely performs the "conjunctive act" doesn't do this. Consider one who entertains and affirms, one by one, a substantial number of propositions, $p_1, \ldots, p_n$, thereby performing the "conjunctive act" of entertaining—and, let us suppose, affirming—all n propositions. Recognizing his or her own fallibility, the agent may have no wish to assert (or deny) their conjunction, which may remain unentertained. Hence the "conjunctive act" is not to be identified with the conjunctive proposition.

In fact, it is no proposition at all because it can't be negated, or operated on by any other operator that forms complex propositions from simpler ones. For the negation operator to apply to a purely representational cognitive act, that act must have a single representational content. The act of (i) entertaining the proposition that o is red, (ii) entertaining the proposition that o* is green, and (iii) applying the conjunctive operation to the two, thereby representing *o as red and o* as green*, satisfies this condition, while the "conjunctive act" of performing (i) and (ii) does not. In applying the negation operation to the result of (iii), one represents things as *not being such that o is red and o* is green*. This illustrates a general point. When I speak of complex propositional acts as representing *so-and-so as being such-and-such*, I am speaking of acts with single representational contents that *may* themselves be arguments of further operations and predications, leading in uniform and systematic ways to further, final acts with single representational contents. Since the "conjunctive act" of predicating being red of o and also predicating being green of o* doesn't have this feature, we can't speak of what the act itself represents in the manner required for it to be a proposition.

Next comes intensional operations on propositions. Performing the operation of *necessitation* on the proposition that represents *A as being F* (and nothing more) gives us the proposition that represents the world as *being such that necessarily A is F* (which may be glossed along deflationary lines similar to those illustrated with negation). In addition, applying the necessitation function to the property *being F* yields the property *being necessarily F*; so applying it to truth yields *being necessarily true*, which can be predicated of any proposition.

Propositions are also made objects of thought when one entertains attitude ascriptions like the proposition that John believes that Kripke isn't Kaplan. This proposition is the act of predicating *belief* of the pair of a pair of arguments the first of which is John (however he is identified) and the second of which is the proposition that Kripke isn't Kaplan, which is identified by entertaining it—i.e., by negating the identity relation to obtain *not being identical*, which is predicated of Kripke (however he is identified) and Kaplan (however he is identified). Other attitude verbs the objects of which are propositions are treated similarly.

Propositions expressed by sentences containing quantifiers can be treated as predicating properties of either complex properties or propositional functions. Although the former may be the more realistic choice, I will here use the latter for ease of exposition. On this model, the proposition *that all Gs are H* is the act of (i) applying the *all*-function to the propositional function g to get the property *being true of all objects to which g assigns a truth*, and (ii) predicating this property of *the propositional function h*.

Sentences containing complex singular terms require us to distinguish two senses of predication. So far, I have spoken only of *direct predication*.

Direct Predication
To *directly predicate* a property P of x is to have x in mind as the thing represented as having P.

Complex singular terms require the relation *mediate predication* holding between an agent, a property, and a function-argument pair *f-plus-y*.

Mediate Predication
To *mediately predicate* P of the complex *f-plus-y* is to aim to (indirectly) represent whatever, if anything, it determines (the value of f at y) as having P.

For example, the proposition *that 6 cubed is greater than 14 squared* is the act of taking 6 as argument of the cubing function, taking 4 as argument of the squaring function, and mediately predicating *being greater than* of *the cubing function plus its argument* followed by *the squaring function plus its argument*. One who performs this predication may be said to *indirectly predicate* being greater than of the pair of numbers, the cube of 6 and the square of 14, determined by the two complexes.

Indirect Predication
Instances of the schema *A indirectly predicates P of T* (where 'P' is replaced by a term standing for a property P* and 'T' is replaced by a complex singular term) express the claim that the agent mediately predicates P* of the propositional content of 'T'.

Not being either direct or mediate predication targets, the numbers that are the cube of 6 and the square of 14 aren't constituents of the proposition. Instead, the pair of function-plus-argument complexes that are *mediate predication targets* of the relation *being greater than* are constituents.

A similar story holds for Fregean definite descriptions, which express function-argument complexes in which the ι-function maps its argument function g onto the unique object to which g assigns a truth, if there is one, and otherwise is undefined. The proposition *that the G is H* is the act of taking g as argument of ι, and mediately predicating *being H* of the complex *ι-plus-g*. Although failure of ι to be defined at g will render the proposition untrue, it won't threaten its existence. Just as one can look for the fountain the waters of which ensure eternal youth, even though there is no such thing, so one can *indirectly predicate* a property of *the G*, even when the ι-function doesn't assign a value to the argument designated by the formula replacing 'G'.

With this distinction, we can solve Russell's "Gray's Elegy puzzle" from "On Denoting" that led him wrongly to conclude that complex singular terms are impossible.[9] The key examples are given in (5), in which 'M' is a Millian name for the meaning of the description, which is assumed for *reductio* to be a singular term.

5a. The first line of Gray's Elegy is 'The curfew tolls the knell of parting day'.

5b. 'The first line of Gray's Elegy' means M.

5c. 'The first line of Gray's Elegy' means the first line of Gray's Elegy.

Since the symbol 'M' is assumed to name the meaning of the phrase 'the first line of Gray's Elegy', Russell reasons that the two expressions

---

[9] Russell (1905). For a revealing reconstruction, see Salmon (2005). Although I lean toward Russell in taking singular definite descriptions in English to be generalized quantifiers, I lean toward Frege in recognizing the legitimacy of complex singular terms conforming to his analysis.

should contribute the same constituent to propositions (5b) and (5c), which, since they have the same structure, should be identical. But they can't be identical; for if the description means M, (5b) should be true, even though (5c) is false, because it identifies the meaning of the description with the thing it denotes. Russell resolves the conflict by embracing R and denying that (5b) expresses a proposition.

R If definite descriptions are singular terms, they express meanings that denote unique objects satisfying them (if such there
   be), which are the targets of predication in propositions expressed by sentences containing them. Thus, these meanings
   can never themselves be predication targets in any proposition in which they occur.

Continuing to suppose, for *reductio*, that descriptions are singular terms, Russell concludes from R that there is no true singular propo- sition in which *being what 'the first line of Gray's Elegy' means* is predi- cated of anything. For him, this ensures that no one can *know of* anything that it is what the description means. But surely, in order for E to mean something it must be possible to know of *what E means* that E means it. So, he concludes, it is impossible for meaningful definite descriptions (of any language) to be singular terms.

The argument, which must be unsound, can be generalized to rule out all complex singular terms, including '2 + 2'. Russell's error in arriving at this false conclusion is in identifying propositions (5b) and (5c). Although they have the same constituents, they don't have the same structure. Since propositions are cognitive acts, the struc- tural relationships their parts bear are the roles they play in the cognitive operations performed by agents who entertain them— roles like *being predicated directly, or indirectly* (of certain things), *being targets* (of certain predications), and the like. The structural difference between (5b) and (5c) is in how their common property is predicated of its arguments. The former is true because it *directly predicates being what 'the first line of Gray's Elegy' means* of the complex M; the latter is false because it *mediately predicates* that property of the complex, and hence *indirectly predicates* that property of what M determines. This distinction—between what one who entertains (5b) *aims to represent* as having a certain property versus what one who entertains (5c) *aims to represent*—is built into cognitive propositions.

What made the distinction between these two proposition undetectable for Russell was his conception of propositions as Platonic entities the intentional properties of which are prior to, and independent of, agents who entertain them. Thinking of propositions in this way, and asking "What does M do in proposition (5c) that it doesn't do in (5b)?," he naturally answered "Nothing!" With cognitive propositions, we ask "What do *agents* use M to do when entertaining proposition (5c) that they don't use it to do when entertaining (5b)?" Since the answer—*stand in for its denotation*—is obvious, what had been a puzzle ceases to be. However, we have not quite reached the bottom of this puzzle. To do so, a further word must be said about how propositions and their constituents are cognized.[10]

COGNITIVE CONDITIONS ON THE CONSTITUTION OF PROPOSITIONS

With this in mind, I turn to distinct but representationally identical propositions like those in (6)–(7).

6a. Russell tried to prove (the proposition) that arithmetic is reducible to logic.

6b. Russell tried to prove logicism.

---

[10] The full story of Russell's reasoning and the instructive errors behind it is told in chapter 8 of Soames (2014b).

7a. Mary believes that Russell tried to prove (the proposition) that arithmetic is reducible to logic.

7b. Mary believes that Russell tried to prove logicism.

Here, 'logicism' is a Millian proper name for the proposition L *that arithmetic is reducible to logic*, designated by the directly referential *that*-clause. Although L is what the two terms contribute to the representational contents of the propositions in (6) and (7), propositions (7a) and (7b) can differ in truth value. If Mary picked up the name 'logicism' by hearing it used to designate some thesis in the philosophy of mathematics that Russell tried to prove, (7b) may be true, even if she has no clue what he thought about arithmetic, in which case (7a) is false. How can this be?[11]

The cognitive conception of propositions tells us. According to it, understanding (6b) and entertaining the proposition it expresses requires predicating *trying to prove* of Russell (however he is identified as predication target) and L (however it is identified). Since one can use the name 'logicism' to identify L without knowing much about its referent, one who has picked up the name can entertain proposition (6b) without being able to identify L in any more informative manner. The conditions for understanding and entertaining (6a) are the same, except that one is required to identify the second predication target, L, by entertaining it (which involves predicating *being reducible* of arithmetic and logic). *So, to entertain proposition (6a) is to entertain proposition (6b), but not conversely*, from which the different truth conditions of (7a) and (7b) follow. *Because propositions are acts of cognizing things and predicating properties of them, propositions p and q can place different constraints on how one who entertains them*

---

[11] This issue was originally addressed in Richard (1993). It is also discussed in Soames (2007c).

cognizes their predication targets, even if the truth conditions of p and q result from predicating the same properties of the same things. Propositions (6a) and (6b) predicate the same property of the same proposition, but only (6a) requires it to be entertained.

This illustrates two aspects of propositional content: representational content (which imposes conditions on the world necessary for truth) and cognitive content (which imposes conditions on agents who entertain it). With this bipartite conception of content, we characterize the meaning of the term 'logicism' as its contribution, L, to the representational content of proposition (6b). The meaning of the clause 'that arithmetic is reducible to logic' consists of that same contribution to representational content *plus* its contribution to the cognitive content of proposition (6a), which requires L to be cognized by entertaining it. Because of this difference, the constituents of L play different roles in propositions (6a) and (6b), even though L itself is a constituent of both.

On this conception, 'logicism' and 'that arithmetic is reducible to logic' directly designate the same proposition, which is itself a constituent of (larger) propositions expressed by sentences containing the terms. Nevertheless, these larger propositions differ in that the clausal term contributes, in addition to its designation, what may be called a *Millian mode of presentation* that requires its designation to be cognized by entertaining it. With this in mind, consider the examples in (8).

8a. Logicism is (the proposition) that arithmetic is reducible to logic.
8b. Logicism is logicism.
8c. That arithmetic is reducible to logic is (the proposition) that arithmetic is reducible to logic.

Each of these propositions is true, all have the same constituents and the same structure, and each is representationally identical to the other two. Nevertheless, the three propositions are (cognitively) different. Whereas *the second argument of the identity relation* in proposition (8a) is identified via a Millian mode of presentation requiring *it* to be entertained (by one who entertains proposition (8a)), proposition (8b) contains no such Millian mode, while in proposition (8c) both arguments of identity are identified via that mode. Moreover, since to entertain, believe, or know proposition (8c) is to entertain, believe, or know the other two as well, each counts as knowable a priori.[12]

If one tries to visualize propositions—e.g., by drawing them on a page or representing them on a graph—it is hard to make sense of this. In representing the propositional constituents pictorially, one would use aspects of the spatial relationships their representations bear to one another to indicate the structure of the proposition, and so to represent what is predicated of what. But since pictorially representing proposition L on the page would require representing its constituents, the representations of the propositions expressed by (6a) and (6b) would be the same. Representing a proposition as visible in this way requires representing its constituents, and the constituents of its constituents, as similarly visible. So if one thought that entertaining a proposition was something like perceiving it in the mind's eye, one would think that to mentally "see" the proposition *that mathematics is reducible to logic* as a constituent of a larger proposition would require mentally "seeing" its constituents too—as *sub-constituents* of the larger proposition. This is how Russell and, I suspect, many others thought, or have thought, of propositions.

The cognitive conception highlights the dangers of this way of thinking. According to it, propositions (6a) and (6b) are

---

[12] The apriority of (8a) will be revisited in chapter 4, where it is argued that the name 'logicism' may itself be associated with its own Millian mode of presentation.

representationally identical because they represent the same things as standing in the same relation R (while representing nothing further); however, the propositions are *cognitively distinct* because only proposition (6a) requires an agent who entertains it to cognize L by entertaining it, which in turn requires the agent to cognize the constituents of L. In the chapters that follow I will generalize this lesson by identifying many other cases of representationally identical but cognitively distinct propositions. These will be used to expand the solution spaces for a variety of fundamental problems in semantics, the philosophy of language, and the philosophy of mind. First, however, I will extract further, subsidiary lessons from Russell's Gray's Elegy puzzle.

MEANING, UNDERSTANDING, AND KNOWLEDGE OF MEANING

The distinction between direct, mediate, and indirect predication falsifies Russell's thesis R by distinguishing the propositions expressed by (5b) and (5c).

R   If definite descriptions are singular terms, they express meanings that denote unique objects satisfying them (if such there be), which are the targets of predication in propositions expressed by sentences containing them. Thus, these meanings can never themselves be predication targets in any proposition in which they occur.

5b. 'The first line of Gray's Elegy' means M.

  c. 'The first line of Gray's Elegy' means the first line of Gray's Elegy.

The discussion of examples (6) and (7) reveals a further misstep in the argument from R to the conclusion that no definite description or other function-argument expression can be a (non-directly referential) complex singular term. The misstep is embedded in that thought that if such an expression were such a term, then it would be impossible to know its meaning M—in the sense of *knowing of* M that it is what the term means—and so, by implication, it would be impossible to understand the expression.

The misstep is not so much in what is asserted as in the implied connection between understanding an expression (whether simple or complex) and knowing of the entity that is its meaning (assuming it has one) that it is the meaning of the expression. This misstep is revealed once we recognize (a) that propositions are the meanings of some sentences and (b) that propositions can be given proper names. Let 'logicism' name the proposition that arithmetic is reducible to logic, which in turn is the meaning of the sentence 'Arithmetic is reducible to logic.' Just as Mary in the scenario involving (6) and (7) could come to truly believe of this proposition that Russell tried to establish it, by virtue of being told "Russell tried to prove logicism," so Maria, who is learning English, could come to truly believe of this proposition that it is the meaning of a certain sentence, by virtue of being told "Logicism is the meaning of the English sentence 'Arithmetic is reducible to logic'." Just as Mary thereby acquired no ability to informatively identify the proposition Russell tried to prove, so Maria thereby acquires no ability to informatively identify the proposition that is the meaning of the English sentence, and so does not understand it.

This is enough to raise serious questions about the relationship, if any, between *understanding an expression E which in fact means M* and *knowing of M that it is the meaning of E, or that E means it.* We have seen that it is possible to have the knowledge without the understanding. It is also possible to have the understanding without the knowledge. I have already emphasized that according to the cognitive conception of propositions, one can entertain, believe, and assert a proposition—say *that Mommy is coming*—without cognizing, or even having the ability to cognize, that proposition. From here, it is a short step to recognizing that no knowledge of propositions is required in order for one to learn to use the words 'is coming' to predicate the property *being one who is coming* of an individual M whom one has learned to pick out using 'Mommy'. A child in this position has acquired the ability to use the sentence 'Mommy is coming' to entertain, assert, and express his or her belief, or even knowledge, *that M is coming*—which may, in the fragmentary language shared with the child's mother, be the meaning (semantic content) of the sentence 'Mommy is coming'. The child *understands* the sentence, even though the child doesn't know anything about the proposition that is its meaning, including that it is the meaning of the sentence. It is not inconceivable that the same could be true of the sentence '2 + 2 = 4' and the proposition that two plus two equals four.

The lesson to be learned is that understanding an expression is *not*, in general, having knowledge of its semantic properties. Rather, understanding is having the ability to use the expression in conventionally expected ways. In the case of a (non-context-sensitive) declarative sentence S, what, in the first instance, is required is the ability to use S to entertain and assert (or deny) the proposition S semantically expresses. Different requirements apply to other kinds of expressions. I will return to this issue in later chapters, where I will argue that the distinction between (i) *understanding* an expression E and (ii) *knowing of* what E means (expresses/stands for) is needed to solve important problems in the philosophy of language and mind.

Thinking of Oneself, the Present Moment, and the Actual World-State

FIRST-PERSON COGNITION AND *DE SE* ATTITUDES

The distinction between representational and cognitive content introduced in chapter 2 makes possible a new analysis of *de se* attitudes involving first-person cognition. One such example, due to John Perry, is the contrast between my belief *that I am making a mess*, as opposed to my belief, of some shopper, *that he is making a mess*, where the shopper in question is the one whose reflection I see in the supermarket's security mirror, who in fact is me.[1] The new analysis springing from the cognitive conception of propositions distinguishes predicating P of an agent A identified as predication target *in the first-person way* from predicating P of A *however identified*. Since doing the first is also doing the second, but not conversely, the acts are different. Since the same property is predicated of the same thing, they are cognitively distinct but representationally identical propositions. This subverts current orthodoxy. Because that orthodoxy takes representationally identical propositions to be absolutely identical, it holds that a *de se* epiphany—*I am the one making a mess*—can't involve coming to believe a *proposition* not previously believed. Either it involves believing an old proposition—*that he is making a mess*—in a new way

---

[1] Perry (1979).

(as John Perry argued), or it involves believing *a property* that one "self-ascribes" (as David Lewis maintained).[2] Though each analysis has virtues, the former fails to respect our conviction that in *de se* cases one believes something new, while the latter founders on the fact that, as Jeff Speaks put it, to believe *truly* is to believe something *true* (which properties like *making a mess* are not).[3] The cognitive analysis transcends this dilemma.

What others call *A's self-ascribing P* is A's believing the proposition that both predicates P of A and requires one who entertains it to identify A as predication target in the first-person way. Let S contain an occurrence of the first-person singular pronoun. Let S(x) result from replacing it with a variable. S(x) is then associated with a property P, which I model *being assigned a truth by the function that assigns to o the proposition expressed by S(x) relative to an assignment of o to 'x'*. Lewis tells us that an agent A who accepts S *self-ascribes* P. I agree, while adding that *to do this is to accept both a proposition of limited accessibility that only A can entertain plus another, representationally identical, proposition that anyone can*. Although Perry tells us something different, I also agree with his claim that A comes to believe, in a new way, a proposition that A already believed. *To this I add: the new way of believing the old proposition is itself a way of believing a "de se proposition" representationally identical to it*. In this way, the cognitive theory subsumes the motivations of the two leading accounts of *de se* attitudes, while capturing the fact that to believe truly is to believe a truth, which Lewis missed, and also the fact that *de se* epiphanies involve coming to believe new things, which Perry missed.[4]

---

[2] Lewis (1979).

[3] Chapter 5 of King, Soames, and Speaks (2014).

[4] I postpone further discussion of the accounts of Lewis, Perry, and others until chapter 9, when I will relate them to the positive views developed here.

The application of this idea to attitude ascriptions is illustrated by (1), which can be used to report *de re* or *de se* beliefs.

1. Every F believes that he or she is G.

    Every x: Fx (x believes that x is G)

On the *de se* understanding, the proposition expressed predicates *assigning a truth to every F* of the function that assigns to each agent A the proposition that predicates *believing* of A and the proposition p that predicates *being G* of A, *requiring one who entertains p to identify A as predication target of G in the first-person way*. The *de re* understanding of (1) is the same except that the proposition p doesn't require *first-person* cognition of A.

The analysis is extended to (2) by taking the antecedent-anaphor relation to introduce a variable-binding relation.

2. *Mary* believes that *she* is in danger.

    λx (x believes that x is in danger) Mary

In using (3a), I assert my belief in the *de se* proposition only I can entertain plus the representationally identical proposition that anyone can.

3a. I believe that I am such-and-such.

My audience can identify both propositions and thereby come to believe that both are true, or that both are false, even though they can entertain only the latter proposition. They may then use the *de se* understanding of (3b) to report my beliefs, while using (3c) to assess them.

3b. *SS* believes that *he* is such-and-such.

3c. That belief is true/false, necessary/contingent.

I can also use (4) to predicate *being believed by Martha to be in danger* of me, identifying myself as predication target in the first-person way.

4. Martha believes that I am in danger.

    λx (Martha believes x is in danger) me

As in other cases, my coming to believe this proposition may provide me with evidence to believe *de se* that I am in danger, even if believing the related *de re* proposition wouldn't.

Having touched on these fundamentals, I turn to a point about semantics and pragmatics. Although I use the first-person singular pronoun to express propositions only I can entertain, my ability to entertain them is not due to my mastery of the linguistic rule that governs it. This can be seen by comparing the *de se* proposition *that I am in danger* with the ordinary proposition *that SS is in danger,* which I may believe in the same (third-person) way that others can. The difference between my believing the later and my believing the former is tied to their roles in motivating action. While I may believe *that SS is in danger* without seeing reason to worry, believing *that I am in danger* gives me immediate cause for concern. This motivationally efficacious way of believing things about oneself is shared by all agents who can think of, and distinguish themselves, from others—whether or not they speak a language. So the ability to entertain and believe first-person propositions can't depend on mastering a linguistic rule.

How, then, is the meaning of the word 'I' related to the first-person way of thinking and believing? The answer begins with the Kaplanesque rule: *A use of 'I' by an agent A directly refers to A.* Since the semantic content of such use is just the agent A, the information semantically encoded by my use of the sentence ⌈I am F⌉ is the same as that encoded by your use of ⌈SS is F⌉. First-person cognition enters when I use the first-person pronoun, *knowing in the first-person way that I am using it.* Combining this knowledge with knowledge of the semantic rule, I can know, *in the first-person way,* that my use of the sentence 'I am in danger' predicates *being in danger of me.* Since this reasoning is available to all, everyone knows that uses of the word 'I' express first-person cognitions. This underwrites *de se* assertions without any semantic rule assigning *de se* semantic content to uses of first-person sentences.

Something similar can be said about the second-person (singular) pronoun 'you', the semantic rule for which is: A use of 'you' by an agent A addressing someone B directly refers to B. Since the semantic content of such use is just B, the information semantically encoded by Martha's use of the sentence ⌈You are F⌉ in addressing me is the same as that encoded by her use of ⌈SS is F⌉. First-person content enters the picture when the agent uses the second-person pronoun *knowing in the first-person way* that he or she is using it. Combining this knowledge with knowledge both of the semantic rule and of the fact that she is addressing me, Martha can be expected to realize *in the first-person way* that her use of the sentence 'You are in danger' to address me predicates *being in danger* of *the person (SS) she is addressing.* Given that I also know the semantic rule for 'you', while knowing *in the first-person way* that Martha has (knowingly) used the word (which she understands) to address me, I can come to know (and Martha can come to know that I know) *in the first-person way* that I am in danger iff what she asserted is true. Here, first-person information about the speaker is *communicated,* and first-person information about the addressee is *imparted,* even though no first-person proposition is either *asserted* or *semantically expressed.*[5]

What about cases in which first-person propositions are asserted by uses of sentences containing the first-person singular pronoun? How, in general, do we extract the *first-person* assertive content in such cases from the *semantic content p of the sentence uttered*? Although there is a general rule, it's not universal because we extract

---

[5] In chapter 4 this account of the relationship between the information carried by uses of the first- and second-person singular pronouns will be used to resolve second-person analogues of standard first-person *de se* puzzles. Chapter 5 extends the same point to demonstrative uses of 'he'/'she'.

first-person content opportunistically. An agent using the first-person pronoun to express a proposition p signals that the agent is thinking of him- or her-self in the first-person way, and so is "self-predicating" some property F made available by p—where to *self-predicate* F is to predicate F of oneself, identifying oneself as predication target in the first-person way, and to *self-ascribe* is to *self-predicate* affirming that predication (and so accepting the *first-person* proposition that predicates F of one).

How do we figure out which property F is? Here is a rule of thumb. Putting aside (certain) attitude ascriptions for the moment, we let the sentence used by agent A be (5a). Its bare semantic content is expressed by (5b) relative to an assignment of A to 'x'.

5a. . . . I . . . I . . .
5b. . . . x . . . x . . .

This content is equivalent to that expressed by (5c).

5c. λx [. . . x . . . x . . .] I

Since to use (5c) would be to self-ascribe the property represented there, one who assertively utters (5a) can typically be taken to be committed to, and even to have asserted, the *first-person* proposition corresponding to (5c), and, thereby, to be committed to its representationally identical *de re* proposition as well.

Next consider (6a,b).

6a. I believe that I am in danger.
6b. Martha believes that I am in danger.

Applying our reasoning gives us self-predications (6a +) and (6b +).[6]

---

[6] In these and following examples I italicize the first-person pronoun as a way of indicating that the propositions represented by these formulas are those in which the properties indicated by the lambda abstracts are predicated of the agent *identified in the first-person way.*

6a+. λx [x believes that x is in danger] *I*

6b+. λx [Martha believes that x is in danger] *I*

These are distinguished from (6a*) and (6b*).

6a*. λx [x believes: λy *(y is in danger)* *I*] *I*

6b*. Martha believes: λx *(x is in danger)* *I*

Look first at (6b*), which does *not* accord with the rule of thumb I
sketched. It represents Martha as believing a proposition about me
that only I can entertain. No one aware that I am not Martha would
interpret my remark in that way. The proper interpretation of what
I assert in uttering (6b) is represented by (6b+). Now go back to
(6a). Although (6a+) and (6a*) are different, in many situations
there will be no contextually important contrast: (6a+) involves
self-predication of property P+, *being an x such that x believes that x
is in danger*; (6a*) represents self-predication of property P*—*being
an x such that x believes in the first-person way that x is in danger*. Although one can have property P+ without having P*, one can't *self-
ascribe* P+ without, in effect, self-ascribing P*. To self-ascribe P+, I
must represent myself *in the first-person way* as *both* the believer and
the one believed to be in danger. So, for me to affirm the *first-person*
proposition represented by (6a+) is tantamount to also affirming
the closely related *first-person* proposition (6a*).

Next consider my uses of the examples in (7).

7a. I believe that my name is 'Scott'.

7b. Scott believes that my name is 'Scott'.

(7a) is just like (6a); utterances of it commit me to the *first-person*
propositions corresponding to (7a+) and (7a*).

7a+. λx [x believes that x's name is 'Scott'] *I*

7a*. λx [x believes: λy (y's name is 'Scott')*I*] *I*

(7b) is like (6b), except that 'Scott' and my use of the first-person pronoun are coreferential, and so contribute the same constituent to the information semantically encoded. If this coreference is obvious to all (me included), my utterance of (7b) will carry the information carried by my utterance of (7a). If it isn't obvious (perhaps even to me), my use of (7b) will express my commitment to the *first-person* proposition represented by (7b+), but *not* to the *first-person* proposition associated with (7b*).

7b+. λx [Scott believes that x's name is 'Scott'] *I*

7b*.   Scott believes: λx *(x's name is 'Scott') I*

For me to affirm the *first-person* proposition (7b+) is for me to self-ascribe the property *being one whom Scott believes to be named 'Scott'*. This proposition is true iff I have the property I self-ascribe—i.e., iff Scott believes of me that my name is 'Scott'. It is both true and believed by me in the first-person way in a situation in which I have amnesia and don't self-ascribe either *being named 'Scott'*, or *being one who believes oneself to be named 'Scott'*, provided that I (Scott) believe *de re* of a certain person (who turns out to be me) that he believes of me that I am named 'Scott'.

In such a situation, I can use (7c) to assert one of the variants below.

7c.   I don't believe that my name is 'Scott'.

7c+. λx [~ x believes: λy *(y's name is 'Scott') I*] *I*

7c*.   ~ (λx [x believes that x's name is 'Scott'] *I*)

7c**. λx [~ x believes that x's name is 'Scott'] *I*

For me to assert the proposition represented by (7c+) is for me to self-ascribe *not believing of SS in the first-person way that SS is named 'Scott'*. In order for me to know this proposition, I must know of myself (in the first-person way) that I don't self-ascribe *being named 'Scott'* (and so don't have the first-person belief that I am so named).

The proposition represented by (7c*) is a little different. For me to assert this proposition is for me to deny the *first-person proposition* that predicates *believing of one that one is named 'Scott'* of me. I will assert this if I have no reason to suspect that I am such a person. The proposition represented by (7c**) makes the risk inherent in (7c*) explicit. Since to assert it is to self-ascribe *not believing of one that one is named 'Scott'*, knowing it to be true requires knowing that I won't turn out to have the property which is its positive counterpart—which I *will* have, if I turn out to be one who *does* believe, of a certain person x, that x is named 'Scott', where x turns out to be me.

Can't I rule this out? You might think I could by checking whom I believe to be named 'Scott'. But, due to my special circumstances in the amnesia ward, this doesn't settle the matter. Having come across autographed books written by Scott-the-novelist, Scott-the-economist, and Scott-the-director-of-the-amnesia-ward where I am presently staying, I believe of each that his name is 'Scott'. Since each book describes the author's earlier experiences as an amnesia patient in this very ward, and since I further believe that amnesia tends to recur, I think I might be one of them, suffering from a relapse. For this reason, I am *not* willing to commit myself to the truth of proposition (7c**) or proposition (7c*), though I am willing to commit myself to the truth of proposition (7c +). Thus, proposition (7c +) is the most natural choice for expressing the content of my assertive utterance of (7c)—though in less extreme situations (7c*) might do as well. Differences like these are not a matter of semantics, but of what it is reasonable to take the speaker to be trying to get across.

These examples illustrate a lesson I will extend in later chapters. There is a larger gap between the semantic content of a sentence in a context and what is asserted by uttering it there than is usually appreciated. *Often, more than semantic content is asserted, and in cases* like *(7c)—the semantic content of which is (7cs)—semantic content isn't asserted* at all.

7cs. ~ [SS believes that SS's name is 'Scott']

In general, the propositions asserted by an utterance are those that a rational, attentive, and well-informed hearer who shares the presuppositions of the conversation and knows its current purpose would take the speaker to be intending to use the utterance to get across. Since these presuppositions standardly include knowledge of the meanings of the expressions used, as well as knowledge of the conversational setting, semantic contents will, typically, be important determinants of assertive contents. But they are far from exclusive determinants.

This is not to say that first-person cognition is never semantically encoded. In discussing examples of the sort indicated by (1) and (2), I noted that sentences of this kind can be used to report either *de re* or *de se* (i.e., first-person) beliefs.

1. Every F believes that he or she is G.
    Every x: Fx (x believes that x is G)
2. *Mary* believes that *she* is in danger.
    λx (x believes that x is in danger) Mary

This may be because the sentences have two different semantic readings in which the pronoun functions as a bound variable, or it may be that only the *de re* understanding is semantically encoded, while the *de se* understanding arises from pragmatic factors. Nothing I have said forces a choice between these options. But it is natural to think there is at least one kind of attitude report in which the first-person character of the attitude is semantically encoded. Whatever may be said about the (a) and (b) sentences in (8) and (9), the (c) sentences are always used to report a *first-person* cognition.

8a. *John* expects that *he* will F.

8b. *John* expects *himself* to F.

8c. *John* expects to F.

8d. *John* expects *PRO* to F.

9a. *Every man here* expects that *he* will F.

9b. *Every man here* expects *himself* to F.

9c. *Every man here* expects to F.

9d. *Every man here* expects *PRO* to F.

This can be captured by treating the unpronounced constituent 'PRO' in the analysis of the (c) sentences both as a bound variable and as semantically encoding the restriction that the attitude reported be an instance of first-person cognition.

TEMPORAL COGNITION AND THE TEMPORAL *DE SE*

Just as for each person p there is a first-person way of cognizing p no one else can use to cognize p, so, for each time t there is a "present-tense" way of cognizing t *at t* that can't be used at other times to cognize t. Suppose I plan to attend a meeting I know will start at t—noon, June 13, 2013. Not wanting to be late, I remind myself of this on the morning of June 13th. Still, when I hear the clock strike noon, I utter (10a), and my behavior changes.

10a. Oh, the meeting starts now!

Coming to believe of t *in the present-tense way* that the meeting starts then motivates me to hurry off. Had I not believed this, I wouldn't have done so, *even though I would have continued to believe, of t, that the meeting starts then.* Like the first-person way of believing, the present-tense way of believing is motivationally efficacious. In both cases coming to believe in the special way is coming to believe something new, as indicated by the *truth* of my report (10b) at t.

10b. I only just realized that the meeting starts now!

For this report to be true, the proposition to which I only just came to bear the *realizing* relation must be one that predicates *starting at t* of the meeting, the entertainment of which requires identifying the predication target t *in the present-tense way*. This is the proposition asserted, *not* semantically expressed. The semantic rule for 'now' tells us that a use of it at t directly refers to t. So the semantic content of the word 'now' at a context the time of which is t is simply t itself, and the semantic content of the sentence (10a) at that context is the proposition *that the meeting starts at t,* which is identical with the proposition encoded by (10c) relative to an assignment of t to the variable 't_u'.

10c. The meeting starts at t_u.

The proposition expressed or asserted by *the utterance of (10a) at t* is a pragmatic enrichment of this *semantically* expressed proposition that can be entertained only by one who performs the relevant predication identifying the argument t in the present-tense way. Thus "present-tense cognition" is no more part of the semantics of 'now' than first-person cognition is part of the semantics of 'I', 'me', or 'mine'. Rather, the association of present-tense cognition with sentences containing 'now' results from knowledge of the semantic rule for 'now' *plus present-tense knowledge,* when using 'now', that one is doing so. Putting these pieces of knowledge together, one comes to know of the time t at which one is using (10a) that one's use predicates *being when the meeting starts* of t, *identifying t in the present-tense way.*

We determine the contents of such assertions in much the same way we determine the contents of *de se* assertions made using first-person sentences. Although tenses introduce some complications, counterparts of the rules of thumb given in the previous section for first-person assertions apply here as well. For example, the interpretations of uses of (11a) and (11b) are (11a+) and (11b+). (Here, 't' is a variable that ranges over moments, 'd(t)' is a singular term that designates the day of the moment to which 't' is assigned, and u_t is the time of utterance.)

11a.   John believes that the meeting is scheduled to start now.

11a+. λt [John believes at t that the meeting is scheduled to start at t] u_t

11b.   A day ago, John believed that the meeting was scheduled to start now.

11b+. λt [John believed at d(t)-minus-1 that the meeting was scheduled to start at t] u_t

The same considerations apply here as applied to first-person cases. In addition, as (11a+) and (11b+) implicitly indicate, ordinary tensed sentences semantically encode propositions, relative to contexts of use, that contain the time of use as a constituent.[7] Although these semantic contents don't include restrictions on the way in which the utterance time must be cognitively identified, utterances of these sentences can express and communicate propositions of limited cognitive access that include such restrictions for the same sorts of reasons that utterances of first-person sentences do. So, the cognitive theory of propositions allows the distinction between representationally identical first- and third-person propositions to be extended to a distinction between representationally identical present-tense and non-present-tense propositions.

That said, there is a difference between the first-person and present-tense cases that should be noted. The time period designated by a use of 'now', or of the present tense, can vary in length depending on the context. If you ask, "Are you hungry yet?" and I

---

[7] This semantic analysis follows Nathan Salmon (1989b).

answer, "Yes, I am hungry now," the referent of 'now' would presumably be the present moment. But if you ask, "What are you
teaching now?" and I answer, "I am teaching a graduate seminar
now," my answer may be correct, even though the present moment
is not one in which I am actively engaged in teaching anything. In
such a case, my use of 'now' may designate a period of time lasting
months, even though I doubt there is a special motivationally efficacious way of cognizing a period of that length. Rather, I suspect,
the target of the special "present-tense" way of cognizing a time is
always centered on the present moment. Nevertheless, sequences
of adjoining moments that are contextually all but indistinguishable from that moment may, in different circumstances, enjoy a
special status.

The point is illustrated by my utterance of (10b).

10b. I only just realized that the meeting starts now!

The proposition asserted is about the time t of utterance designated
by my use of 'now', cognized in the special present-tense way. What
time was that exactly? Clearly it included the exact *instant of utterance*. But recognizing that it may have included more may help explain a relevant fact: I wouldn't have uttered (10b) had I not lost
track of the time (even if for only a few minutes) prior to coming to
my realization about the meeting.[8] Had I been tracking the time
minute by minute before noon, when I knew the meeting would
begin, I would *not* have been willing to assert that I hadn't, prior to
a moment ago, "realized that the meeting starts *now*."

Why not? The answer, as I see it, rests on four points: (i) the *time
t* designated by my use of 'now' in uttering (10b) was a *(brief) period*
that included at least a few minutes before *the instant of utterance*;
(ii) during the early part of t I had lost track of the time and didn't

---

[8] Thanks to Barbara Partee for pointing out the need to explain this.

anticipate the imminent start of the meeting; (iii) had I not lost track of the time, I would, in the early part of t, have counted as identifying t (the period in question) as predication target of *the meeting starts at* in the present-tense way, thereby realizing in the present-tense way that the meeting started then; (iv) what I (truly) asserted in uttering (10b) was that I had *not*, until very close to the instant of utterance, so identified t as predication target, and hence so realized, in the present-tense way, that the meeting started then.

Examples like this illustrate a respect in which the semantics and pragmatics of 'now' include complications quite different from anything we find with the first-person singular pronoun. Nevertheless, the crucial point remains. Both the pronoun and the temporal indexical are very often used to assert propositions the cognitive contents of which require restricted and special motivationally efficacious forms of cognition that are not required by the representationally identical singular propositions that are the semantic contents of the sentences uttered in the corresponding contexts.

Cognizing the Actual World-State

Representationally identical propositions, it will be recalled, predicate the same properties of the same things, and so represent the world in exactly the same ways. Since propositions are complex, purely representational cognitive acts, the manner in which their subacts are performed may differ in significant ways, with the result that it is sometimes possible for agents to entertain, believe, or know one of a pair of representationally identical propositions without bearing these attitudes to the other. So far, I have recognized three cognitively significant restrictions on propositions that may have this result. The first—which is used to distinguish proposition (12a) from proposition (12b)—requires one who entertains the former, but not the latter, to identify its propositional predication target by entertaining it.

12a. Russell attempted to establish *that arithmetic is reducible to logic*.

12b. Russell attempted to establish *logicism*.

The second restriction—used to distinguish the proposition *that I am in danger* (which I, Scott, now assert by uttering 'I am in danger') from the proposition *that Scott is in danger*—requires one who entertains the first proposition, but not the second, to identify its predication target in the first-person way. The third restriction—used to distinguish the proposition asserted by an utterance at t of 'The meeting starts now' from the semantic content of 'The meeting starts at u_t' relative to an assignment of t to 'u_t'—requires one who entertains the first, but not the second, proposition to identify t as predication target in the present-tense way. In none of these cases does the required cognition involve predicating new content of anything. This is a general feature of propositional restrictions on how their sub-acts are to be performed. Thus, adding such restrictions to propositions that don't themselves involve attitude ascriptions doesn't change representational content (whereas adding them to the propositional object of an attitude ascription typically will change such content).

There is reason to believe that these observations can be extended to include distinct but representationally identical propositions about world-states. Elsewhere, I have argued that a world-state is a property attributable to the universe of making true a set of basic propositions that tells a complete world story (that answers all questions relevant to a contextually determined inquiry).[9] Let 'n' be a simple proper name of w, let 'PW' be a term '*the property making it true that S_1, that S_2, that S_3, etc.*' that designates w by articulating the basic propositions that define w, and let p be a proposition. For p to

[9] The argument, summarized in chapter 6 of Soames (2010a), was originally presented in Soames (2007a).

be true at w is for p to be an *a priori* consequence of the basic propositions used to define w.[10]

With this in mind, consider (13a) and (13b).

13a. The proposition that S is true at PW.
13b. The proposition that S is true at n.

The relationship between the propositions expressed by sentences (13a) and (13b) is like the relationship between the propositions about logicism expressed by sentences (12a) and (12b). In both cases, the paired propositions predicate the same properties of the same things; the first proposition differs from the second only in restricting what it takes to entertain it. Entertaining proposition (12a) requires identifying its constituent, the proposition *that arithmetic is reducible to logic,* by entertaining it; entertaining proposition (13a) requires identifying its constituent, the world-state designated by PW, by entertaining its several propositional sub-constituents. In both cases, 12 and 13, *one who believes the first proposition thereby believes the second, but not conversely.* So, when S expresses a contingent proposition that is both knowable only a posteriori and true at the actual world-state by virtue of being an a priori consequence of the propositions that define it, proposition (13a) is knowable a priori. Since knowing that proposition without justifying empirical evidence guarantees knowing proposition (13b) without such evidence, it follows that the latter is also *knowable a priori,* even if the only knowledge we actually have of it is a posteriori.[11]

Next, we move to indexical uses of 'actually'. Uses of (13c) predicate *being true at* of the pair consisting of the proposition p expressed by S and the actual world-state @.

---

[10] It is not required that the propositions in terms of which a world-state is defined exist at w.

[11] See Soames (2007a, 2010a).

13c. *Actually* S. / The proposition that S is true *at this very world-state*.

A use of (13c) involves identifying the predication target @ as *this very world-state* (which is instantiated and experienced)—on analogy with thinking of the present moment as *this very time* (which one is experiencing). Elsewhere I have argued that when the actual world-state is identified in this way, one can know (13c+) a priori, even when p (expressed by S) is itself knowable only a posteriori.

13c+. Actually S iff S. / The proposition that S is true at this very world-state iff S.

From this result plus the apriority of (13a), it follows that that apriority is not closed under a priori consequence, or even under conjunction.[12]

Should we conclude that uses of (13b) and (13c) express cognitively different but representationally identical propositions? The case that they do parallels those involving the first person and the present tense. I might know, of a world-state n, which turns out to be @, *that at n I will soon be in danger*, without feeling concerned. If I later come to think, *"Actually, or, at this very world-state, I will soon be in danger,"* my behavior will change. Asked to explain why, it seems that I could truly say, *"I only just now realized that actually, or, at this very world-state, I will soon be in danger."* Since this classic *de se* form of argument seems as compelling here as it did in earlier cases, there is reason to think we should conclude that (13b) and (13c) express cognitively distinct but representationally identical propositions, related in the now familiar way.

[12] Soames (2007a, 2010a).

Still, the parallel with the first person and present tense isn't complete. Since propositional objects of attitudes that motivate action *aren't*, in general, indexed for world-states, thinking of @ as *this very world-state* isn't motivationally special in quite the way that first-person and present-tense cognitions are. I am motivated to fight or flee, when I think that *I*—rather than SS—*am*—rather than *was*—in danger. Thought about the actual world-state needn't come into it.

There are, of course, motivational contrasts involving examples like (14).

14a. At PW, I am in danger now.

14b. At n, I am in danger now.

14c. At this very world-state, I am in danger now.

Typically, accepting (a) or (b) won't motivate action unless it also involves accepting (c). But this doesn't show that the indexical 'this very world-state' is motivationally essential in John Perry's special sense, because accepting (d) and believing the world-state-neutral proposition I use it to express is sufficient to motivate me to act.

14d. I am in danger now.

Indeed the motivational force associated with accepting (14c), and believing the proposition I use it to express, is due to the transparent connection between (14c) and (14d). In short, even though there is a special way of cognizing a world-state w at w, such cognition isn't essential for motivation and action.[13]

WHERE WE STAND

In chapter 1 I argued that a new conception of propositions as pieces of information is needed, if we are to continue to make progress in semantics, the philosophy of language, and the philosophy of mind. In

---

[13] This transition is explained in Soames (2010a), pp. 134–35.

chapter 2, I outlined the cognitive conception of propositions and argued for its metaphysical and epistemic virtues. These included (i) its resolution of the problem of the unity of the proposition, construed as that of explaining how propositions can be representational and hence bearers of truth and falsity; (ii) its explanation of how cognitive agents—sophisticated or unsophisticated, language-using or not—can believe and bear other attitudes to propositions they either do not cognize or are not capable of cognizing; (iii) its explanation of when knowledge of propositions is required and how it is achieved; (iv) its account of how a proposition can exist even if one or more of its constituents don't exist; (v) its identification of propositions as conceptually prior to the notions of truth and world-states, and hence available to help explain those notions rather than presupposing them; and (vi) its explanation of what the truth of a proposition amounts to, of how its truth conditions are read off it, of why those truth conditions don't vary from world-state to world-state, and of why a proposition need not exist at a world-state in order to be true at that state.

I also pointed out how the conception of propositions as purely representational cognitive acts allows us (a) to distinguish the conditions a proposition imposes on the world if it is to be as the proposition represents it to be from the conditions it imposes on agents who entertain it, and (b) to identify pairs of cognitively distinct but representationally identical propositions. In addition to being relevant to understanding and resolving Russell's Gray's Elegy problem, (a) and (b) were crucial in explaining the semantic difference between articulated, but directly referential, terms like 'that arithmetic is reducible to logic' and simple directly referential terms like 'logicism', and hence in explaining why some attitude ascriptions that differ only in the substitution of one of these two terms for the other differ in truth value.

The burden of chapter 3 has been to sketch new solutions to problems in semantics, the philosophy of language, and the philosophy of mind that the cognitive conception of propositions makes possible when combined with special features of first-person cognition, present-tense cognition, and cognition of the actual state of the world as *this very world-state*. The key has been to expand our recognition of the range of cognitively distinct but representationally identical propositions generated by the two faces of the content of cognitive propositions. Chapters 4 and 5 will be devoted to the explanatory benefits of still further expansions. The general thesis to be defended is that *just as structured propositions make analyses available that are wrongly excluded when propositions are identified with sets of possible world-states, so cognitive propositions make needed analyses available that are excluded by traditional accounts of structured propositions.*

Linguistic Cognition, Understanding, and Millian Modes of Presentation

In chapters 2 and 3, I discussed four forms of cognition that may be incorporated into singular propositions as the means by which one identifies targets of direct predication. They are: entertaining a proposition that is itself a predication target (or a constituent of such a target), first-person cognition, present-tense cognition, and cognition of the actual world-state as *this very state*. Each involves identifying a propositional constituent by performing a sub-act which involves a special way of cognizing it. Each is, therefore, what philosophers of language since Frege have called a "mode of presentation." However, these are *not* Fregean modes of presentation because (i) many propositions are entirely free of such modes of presentation, and (ii) these new modes of presentation do not affect representational content. For these reasons, I call them "Millian modes of presentation." The presence of a particular Millian mode M does, of course, distinguish a proposition p_M incorporating M from an otherwise identical proposition p_{M*} in which a different Millian mode M* is swapped for M; the presence of M also distinguishes p_M from an otherwise identical proposition p that does not incorporate any mode of presentation for what M presents. The upshot is that these three propositions are cognitively distinct, despite being representationally identical.

There are other, related, differences between Millian and Fregean modes of presentation. On the classical picture, a Fregean mode of presentation is epistemically prior to what it represents in the sense of being something that is directly before one's mind, which, when it occurs as a constituent in a proposition, has the function of uniquely determining something else that itself counts as cognized in a related sense (despite not being a constituent of the proposition). The Fregean determination relation is held to be objective in the sense that what, if anything, a mode of presentation determines depends only on it, not on who is cognizing it or whether it is cognized at all. Thus, it is impossible for the same mode of presentation to determine different things relative to the same circumstance of evaluation. If nothing is uniquely determined, the proposition containing the mode of presentation continues to exist unaffected, and to hence be available as an object of the attitudes, despite perhaps failing to be true or false. When Fregean propositions are replaced by cognitive propositions, the nearest analogues of Fregean modes of presentation are the function-argument complexes identified in chapter 2 as the semantic contents of complex singular terms. Their role as constituents of propositions and determinants of representational content is to present indirect predication targets, which, though not themselves constituents of propositions, are crucial to evaluating their truth or falsity.

Millian modes of presentation are different. Since they are neither constituents of a proposition nor what those constituents represent, they are neither cognized in entertaining a proposition nor relevant to determining its truth conditions or truth value. Rather, they are the means by which what is both cognized and constitutive of representational content is brought to mind. Consider again first-person cognition. The complex cognitive act that is the proposition expressed by (1a) differs from the corresponding act that is the proposition I alone can express using (1b).

1a. SS is in danger.

1b. I am in danger.

The former is the act of predicating *being in danger* of the predication target SS (with no restriction on how SS is brought to mind); the latter is an otherwise identical act except that SS is brought to mind *in the first-person way*. In the second case, the sub-act of identifying the predication target in the first-person way is one of several possible methods of doing so. For a proposition p to incorporate this first-person Millian mode of presentation is for it to occur as a sub-act of p. Since the predication target is determined by the first-personal sub-act performed *plus* the identity of the agent performing it, the same first-person mode occurs in the first-person propositions expressed by different agents. Thus it is quite different from any Fregean mode of presentation.

Analogous remarks apply to *present-tense* cognition of t and *this-very-world-state* cognition of w. The Millian modes of presentation for these cases are, respectively, the sub-act of cognizing a moment of time t at t in the present-tense way and the sub-act of cognizing a world-state w at a world-state w in the this-very-world-state way. Finally, consider again propositions (2a) and (2b).

2a. Russell attempted to establish that arithmetic is reducible to logic.

2b. Russell attempted to establish logicism.

The latter proposition is the act of predicating *attempting to establish* of Russell (however identified) and the proposition logicism (however identified); the former is the same except that the proposition logicism must be identified by entertaining it. Having clarified the notion of a Millian mode of presentation and illustrated the role it plays in generating cognitively distinct but representationally identical propositions, I will argue in this chapter that *linguistic modes of presentation* are included among the Millian modes.

It is a feature of language not only that it allows us to share our antecedent nonlinguistic cognitions with others, but also that it is the means by which we perform many cognitions in the first place. For example, many names and natural kind terms we employ designate items with whom or with which we have had little or no perceptual contact. When we identify these items as targets either of predication or of other cognitive operations, we do so linguistically. The same is true even of things with which we have had some perceptual contact; many of our thoughts about them are linguistically mediated—as are some of our thoughts about those with whom, or with which, we are very familiar. Learning a language is, at bottom, learning to use its sentences to entertain the propositions they express, which is to *perform* those propositions. One who understands the sentence 'Plato was human' has learned to use it to predicate humanity of Plato. We use the name 'Plato' to pick out the man, the noun 'human' to pick out the kind, and the phrase 'is human' to predicate *being human* of the man.

Now notice an interesting fact. Let S express p, which is a certain cognitive act. The act *using S to perform p* is itself a cognitive act that is representationally identical to p. If this new representational act is itself a proposition p*, then it is cognitively distinct from, but representationally identical to, p. Is it a proposition? Not all representational acts are. For example, the acts of *predicating humanity of Plato* (i) *on Thursday,* (ii) *in Peru,* (iii) *while dancing,* (iv) *in giving a lecture,* or (v) *when speaking in a whisper* all represent Plato as being human, even though we would not be happy thinking of them as propositions. We can exclude them by insisting that propositions be *purely representational* acts, while observing that these unwanted

examples all involve something further that is representationally irrelevant. The principle expressed by (3) is a corollary of this idea.

3. If A is a cognitive act that is a proposition, and B is a special
    way of performing A that is representationally identical to A
    (so that every conceivable performance of B is a performance
    of A, but not conversely), then B is a proposition only if it
    differs from A solely by containing one or more cognitive
    sub-acts the performance of which are *the means* by which
    one or more of the essential sub-acts of A are performed—
    e.g., by containing sub-acts the performance of which are the
    means by which one or more of the constituents of A are
    identified, so that one identifies the relevant constituents *by*
    performing those sub-acts.

This criterion excludes the unwanted proposition candidates just
cited. For example, let A be the act of predicating humanity (however
cognized) of Plato (however cognized), and let B be the act of doing
this while dancing. Any agent who performs either one of these acts
represents Plato as being human, and nothing more; so the two acts
are representationally identical. However, since dancing is not a cognitive means by which one identifies Plato as predication target, B is
not a proposition, even though A is. Not being a proposition, B is not
the object of propositional attitudes. Although whether or not one is
dancing at t may causally influence what one is thinking at t, the
mere fact that one is dancing isn't a constitutive determinant of either
the representational or the cognitive content of one's beliefs or other
cognitive attitudes. By contrast, (3) does not disqualify predicating
being in danger of me, cognized in the first-person way, from counting
as a proposition; nor does it disqualify (i) predicating *starting now* of
the meeting and the present time, identifying the latter in the present-
tense way, or (ii) predicating *trying to prove* of Russell and logicism,

identifying the latter by entertaining it. The principle expressed by (3) also accommodates predicating *being human* of Plato by using the name 'Plato' to identify the man, the noun 'human' to identify the property, and the phrase 'is human' to predicate the property of the man. Since this act of using the sentence 'Plato is human' to predicate humanity of Plato also satisfies the conditions given in chapter 2 that are necessary for representational acts to be propositions, it *is* a proposition that is cognitively distinct from but representationally identical to the bare proposition that Plato is human.

The point is general. Whenever the conditions in (3) are satisfied and we adopt a special purely representational means of entertaining a proposition p, we generate a new proposition p* representationally identical to p. In the first-person case we noticed that one means of identifying SS as the predication target of *being in danger* involves cognizing SS in the first-person way. Since this second act is purely representational, it is also a proposition. Since not all performances of the first act are performances of the second, they are *different* but representationally identical. Since every performance of the second act is a performance of the first act, entertaining the second proposition counts as entertaining the first, but not conversely. The same is true with linguistic cognition. Here, we start with the act *predicating humanity (however it is cognized) of Plato (however he is cognized)*. One way of performing this act is to use the words 'is human' to predicate humanity of the man picked out using his name. Since both acts are purely representational, both are propositions. Since not all performances of the first are performances of the second, they are *different* but representationally identical. Still, every performance of the second is a performance of the first; so entertaining the second, linguistically enhanced, proposition counts as entertaining the first, but not conversely.

It will be noticed that this account generates a great many previously unrecognized linguistically enhanced propositions. This vast domain includes not only propositions incorporating complete sentences as ways of entertaining otherwise bare propositions, but all sorts of hybrids as well—e.g., the partially enhanced proposition that predicates humanity (however cognized) of the individual Plato one cognizes by using his name. Although the possibilities are virtually endless, I am not multiplying entities. The acts are real. One *can* predicate humanity of Plato; one can also do so by cognizing humanity in this or that way, and cognizing Plato using these or those words. The acts are cognitively different, though representationally identical. Calling them 'propositions' doesn't inflate one's ontology.

The real question is whether the species of representational cognitive acts I have identified can do the work traditionally reserved for propositions. In chapter 2, I argued that they can. I then expanded the case to include several kinds of *propositions of limited access* cognitively distinct from, but representationally identical to, *propositions of unlimited access*. As I argued earlier, the case for recognizing these propositions of limited access is not diminished by the fact that some of them—e.g., the "degenerate" proposition that Martha believes a proposition that only I can entertain—may be of little use to us. The same can be said about some "degenerate" propositions concerning times and world-states. Thus, it should be no surprise that many in the vast domain of possible *linguistically enhanced propositions* may be at most marginally useful to us in constructing theories of language and mind. But this hardly shows that none are. In what follows, I will argue that linguistically enhanced propositions play an important role in solving long-standing problems.

NAMES, FREGE'S PUZZLE, AND LINGUISTIC MODES OF PRESENTATION

I begin with puzzle cases involving names. For each name (or set of such), there are purely representational acts, *propositions*, distinguishable from their representationally identical counterparts by the fact that performing them requires agents to identify predication targets using that name. All these propositions are purely representational acts, all are assigned truth conditions in the usual way, and all are potential objects of attitudes like entertaining, judging, and believing. With this in mind, consider (4).

4a. Carl Hempel was a famous philosopher.

4b. Peter Hempel was a famous philosopher.

4c. x was a famous philosopher (relative to an assignment of Mr. Hempel as value of 'x').

Let p be expressed by (4c). P_C is a proposition representationally identical to p that requires one who entertains it to identify Mr. Hempel via the name 'Carl Hempel'. P_P requires identification via the name 'Peter Hempel'. Utterances of (4a) assert both P_C and p; utterances of (4b) assert P_P and p. With these elementary observations we reconcile a pair of heretofore hard-to-combine insights: one who accepts (4a) may, as Frege noted, believe something different from what one believes in accepting (4b), even though the propositions believed are representationally identical, as intimated by Kripke.

The difference between the two propositions—P_C and P_P—is a difference in how Mr. Hempel is presented, or, as Frege would put it, in "modes of presentation" of Mr. Hempel. What Frege missed, because of his other-worldly conception of propositions, is that these modes are *ways doing things*, e.g., identifying predication targets, which need not be constituents of the representational content of the thing done, the proposition, and so need not affect its truth conditions. Just as structured propositions open up needed analyses of attitudes that are artificially foreclosed when propositions are taken to be sets of possible world-states, so cognitive propositions open up analyses artificially foreclosed by traditional conceptions of structured propositions.

Here is a personal example. Shortly after arriving at Princeton as an Assistant Professor in 1980, I encountered a distinguished gentleman whom others called 'Peter Hempel'. Months later I discovered he was the famous philosopher Carl Hempel. Then, I could have truly reported my epistemic state using (5a), despite the fact I could not very well have done so with (5b).

5a. I have only just now realized that Peter Hempel is the famous philosopher Carl Hempel.
5b. I have only just now realized that Carl Hempel is the famous philosopher Carl Hempel.

The truth I would then have reported is that I hadn't, until recently, known or believed the enhanced proposition entertained by predicating the identity relation of Mr. Hempel, identified using the name 'Peter Hempel', and Mr. Hempel, identified using the name 'Carl Hempel' (even though I had believed the corresponding bare singular proposition). Pressed to explain what it was, precisely, that I hadn't previously grasped, I would probably have answered along the lines of (5c).

5c. I have only just now realized that the man, Mr. Hempel, previously known to me as 'Peter Hempel' is the famous philosopher Carl Hempel, known to me as 'Carl Hempel'.

Although this would have been true, and may in some conversational settings even have been among the propositions asserted by my utterance of (5a), it is inferentially downstream from the truth directly reported by my use of (5a).

It is crucial in considering (4) and (5) to distinguish (i) predicating *being so-and-so* of o using a name n as one's means of designating, and so identifying, o from (ii) predicating both *being so-and-so* and *being named n* of o. Doing the former doesn't involve doing the latter; so one who asserts the proposition that is the first cognitive act need not assert the proposition that is the second. Since the two propositions predicate different properties of o, and so represent o differently, they have different truth conditions. The former is true at world-state w iff o is so-and-so at w; the truth of the latter also requires n to be used at w to designate o.

The case illustrated by (5a) is further generalized in (6) and (7).[1]

6a. John asserts/believes that Carl Hempel was a famous philosopher.

6b. John asserts/believes that Peter Hempel was a famous philosopher.

7a. John didn't assert/believe that Carl Hempel was a famous philosopher.

7b. John didn't assert/believe that Peter Hempel was a famous philosopher.

When it is presupposed that one's audience knows that John is familiar with Mr. Hempel under the name 'Carl Hempel', one may use (6a) to attribute to John assertion of, or belief in, a proposition that requires the predication target, Mr. Hempel, of *being a famous philosopher* to be identified using that name, while using (7a) to deny that attribution. Similarly for (6b), (7b), and the name 'Peter Hempel'. When it isn't presupposed that John knows Mr. Hempel by name, there is no similar enrichment.

For example, I might correctly use (8) to report John's inquiry, even though he didn't know, or use, Martha's name.

8.   John asked whether Martha was my wife.

---

[1] For related discussion, see Soames (2005b) and chapters 6 and 8 of Soames (2002).

Here, the proposition I use the complement clause to contribute to the proposition I assert is *not* one the entertainment of which *requires* an agent to identify its predication target by name. This might be problematic if the proposition *semantically encoded* by the clause required one who entertained it to use 'Martha'. But it doesn't.

There are, of course, many cases of both kinds: those in which linguistic information about the use of names by agents of reported attitudes is presupposed, and those in which it isn't. This variation, which has been the bane of attempts to give semantic solutions to Frege's puzzle, suggests that propositions *semantically expressed* by sentences containing names don't require agents who entertain them to pick out their constituents in any special linguistic way. Linguistic enhancements are simply candidates for pragmatic enrichment. In short, the cognitive theory of propositions allows us to incorporate some of what Nathan Salmon calls "guises" (by which propositional constituents are picked out in entertaining them) into propositions themselves, without changing representational content, and without semantic encoding.[2]

With this in mind, I revisit a classic instance of Frege's puzzle.

9a.   Peter Hempel is Peter Hempel.

9b.   Peter Hempel is Carl Hempel.

10a. Mary knows that Peter Hempel is Peter Hempel.

10b. Mary knows that Peter Hempel is Carl Hempel.

Although the semantics of the (a) sentences are the same as those of the (b) sentences, the propositions they are used to assert are typically different. One who assertively utters (9b) asserts a set of

---

[2] Salmon (1986). Since typically such guises are not included in semantic content, Salmon and I continue to agree on the semantic contents of the sentences in question, even if we disagree regarding which propositions are asserted by utterances of sentences containing names and other singular terms.

distinct but representationally identical propositions, each of which predicates identity of the pair of Mr. Hempel and Mr. Hempel. One of these places no restrictions on how the arguments of the identity relation are identified; one requires only that the first argument be identified using the name 'Peter Hempel', one requires only that the second argument be identified using 'Carl Hempel'; and one requires both. Typically the reason for uttering (9b) is to assert and convey this last proposition—along with, in some cases, further representational-content–changing enrichments of it.

For example, if it is already presupposed in the context that 'Carl Hempel' designates a famous philosopher and that 'Peter Hempel' designates the man to whom you have just been introduced, I may answer your question "Who is the man, Peter Hempel, to whom I have just been introduced?" by uttering (9b), "Peter Hempel is Carl Hempel." In such a case, I thereby assert the proposition that predicates *being identical* of a pair of arguments the first of which is Mr. Hempel, *identified using 'Peter Hempel'*, and the second of which is Mr. Hempel, *identified using 'Carl Hempel'*. Because of the special circumstances of the context of utterance, I will also communicate, and might also be counted as asserting, the further descriptively enriched proposition *that the man, Mr. Hempel (identified using 'Peter Hempel'), to whom you have been introduced is the famous philosopher, Mr. Hempel (identified using 'Carl Hempel')*. Although the first pragmatically enriched proposition is representationally identical to the bare singular proposition semantically expressed by the sentence uttered, the second enriched proposition changes representational content by adding further conditions that Mr. Hempel must satisfy if the proposition is to be true.

All of this carries over to assertive utterances of the attitude ascription (10b). As before, the proposition semantically expressed is uninteresting. So, speakers use, and hearers expect them to use, the sentence to attribute knowledge to Mary of an enrichment of its complement clause. One minimal enrichment merely adds linguistic restrictions on how the arguments of the identity relation are identified. Although this enrichment is representationally inert, the perspective it provides on Mary's cognition may allow hearers to infer further, asserted or unasserted, contents about what Mary knows. If she is known to be a philosophy of science student who will recognize the name 'Carl Hempel', and to be one to whom Mr. Hempel has been introduced as 'Peter Hempel', then the utterance of (10b) will put hearers in a position to infer that she knows that Mr. Hempel, to whom she has been introduced as 'Peter Hempel', is the philosopher of science Carl Hempel, who publishes under that name. In some contexts, this might be included in what is asserted. But whatever Mary is *asserted* to know in a given case will often be supplemented by further information the conveyance of which the linguistic enrichments have facilitated.

Apriority, Aposteriority, and Representational Identity

This sort of enrichment also adds a new twist to discussions of the apriority or aposteriority of propositions expressed by identity sentences containing Millian names. The bare singular proposition p that is the semantic content of both (9a) and (9b) (which predicates identity of Mr. Hempel and Mr. Hempel) is knowable a priori because there are ways of entertaining it—e.g., by performing the predication recognizing the use of the same name 'Peter Hempel' twice over—such that, once entertained, no empirical evidence is needed to justify accepting the proposition, or to determine it to be true. Descriptive enrichments such as the proposition that *the man, Mr. Hempel, to whom you have been introduced is the famous philosopher, Mr. Hempel* are, of course, knowable only a posteriori. What about the minimal enrichment of the semantic content of (9a) and (9b) that requires the first and second arguments of the identity relation to be identified using the names 'Peter Hempel' and 'Carl Hempel' respectively?

Although this proposition—call it "P_{PC}"—is representationally identical to the a priori truth p semantically expressed by (9a) and (9b), it is knowable only a posteriori. When one entertains P_{PC}, one has no way of determining its truth by reflection, without being provided with empirical information that the names are being used codesignatively. What has, until now, made the aposteriority of P_{PC} difficult for Millians like Salmon and me to recognize has been our tendency, along with almost everyone else, to take representationally identical propositions to be absolutely identical. With cognitive propositions, one can see how the linguistically enriched proposition P_{PC} associated with (9b) can be representationally identical to the a priori truth p semantically expressed by (9a), without itself being knowable a priori. But one must be careful how one expresses this. *If,* when one asks, *"Is the proposition that Peter Hempel is Carl Hempel knowable a priori?,"* one is asking whether the proposition p *semantically expressed* by (9b) is knowable a priori, then the answer is, as Salmon and I have long maintained, "Yes." But if one is asking whether the linguistically enriched proposition P_{PC} that sentence (9b) is often used to express is knowable a priori, then the answer is "No, it isn't."

With this we can add an addendum to the discussion of the following trio of propositions characterized in chapter 2 as distinct, representationally identical truths distinguished by the presence, absence, or distribution of the Millian mode of presentation requiring one or more of the arguments of the identity relation to be identified by entertaining it.

11a. Logicism is (the proposition) that arithmetic is reducible to logic.

11b. Logicism is logicism.

11c. That arithmetic is reducible to logic is (the proposition) that arithmetic is reducible to logic.

In that discussion I took 'logicism' to contribute only its referent to the propositions expressed by (11a) and (11b). On that understanding (11a) counted as knowable a priori, by virtue of the fact that knowledge of proposition (11c) was sufficient for knowledge of (11a). But if we consider a case in which the proposition an agent uses (11a) to present is one in which the first argument of the identity relation is identified using the name 'logicism', then the proposition presented is knowable only a posteriori.

Linguistic Modes of Presentation and Kripke's Puzzle

Typically in philosophy we have assumed that we can uniquely specify propositions using constructions of the form *the proposition that S*, when S is unambiguous and indexical-free. We have assumed that uses of 'the proposition that Hesperus is Phosphorus' and 'the proposition that London is pretty' each designate a single proposition that doesn't vary from use to use. The reality of free linguistic enhancement and other pragmatic enrichment belies this in a way that connects with an observation made in Kripke (1979). There, Kripke introduces a formerly monolingual Frenchman, Pierre, who moves to London and learns English by immersion, without learning that 'Londres' translates 'London', and hence without learning that 'Londres est jolie' translates 'London is pretty'. Although Pierre understands the former as well as any monolingual Frenchman, while understanding the latter as well as any monolingual Englishman, he sincerely assents to the former while sincerely dissenting from the latter. Kripke asks "Does Pierre believe that London is pretty, or not?" The answer he wants is a simple "Yes" or "No," not a redescription of Pierre's cognitive situation in other terms. Refusing to provide such an answer himself, Kripke argues that any direct answer faces seemingly disqualifying difficulties.

He says:

> I have no firm belief as to how to solve it [the puzzle]. But beware of one source of confusion. It is no solution in itself to observe that some *other* terminology, which evades the question whether Pierre believes that London is pretty, may be sufficient to state all the relevant facts. I am fully aware that complete and straightforward descriptions of the situation are possible and that in this sense there is no paradox. . . . But none of this answers the central question. Does Pierre, or does he not, believe that London is pretty? I know of no answer to *this* question that seems satisfactory.[3]

Later, he adds the following suggestive diagnosis of the source of the problem he has exposed.

> When we enter into the area exemplified by . . . Pierre our normal practices of interpretation and attribution of belief are subjected to the greatest possible strain, perhaps to the point of breakdown. So is the notion of the *content* of someone's assertion, the *proposition* it expresses.[4]

---

[3] Kripke (1979), at pp. 895–96 of the 1997 reprinting.
[4] Ibid., 906.

Using cognitive conception of propositions, we can identify what has broken down, and why.

Our normal practices of interpretation and belief attribution allow us to use meaning-preserving translations in interpreting the words of others and ascribing beliefs to them. The resulting reports contain *that*-clauses which we take to uniquely specify the proposition believed. But sometimes in moving from one language to another, the loss of words used to express propositions results in the loss of propositions we need or wish to express. There are, of course, many propositions we can express in one language when describing attitudes of speakers of another. But there are also linguistically enhanced propositions representationally identical to their linguistically neutral counterparts that play crucial roles in the lives of agents like Pierre. In his case, we have no way, without using or mentioning French words, to report some of his motivationally significant beliefs.

Because of this we have a hard time answering Kripke's question, "Does Pierre believe that London is pretty?," with a simple "Yes" or "No"—even though we can say precisely what Pierre does, and doesn't, believe. He believes the proposition semantically expressed by 'Londres est jolie' and 'London is pretty', which simply predicates *being pretty* of London. He also believes the proposition semantically expressed by their negations. He further believes the enhanced proposition that predicates *being pretty* of London, entertainable only by one who identifies London via the name 'Londres'; he does *not* believe its negation. The situation is reversed for the enhancement of the semantic content of 'London is pretty' entertainable only by identifying London via the name 'London'.

The reason that neither this nor any other story will provide a simple answer to Kripke's question is that he hasn't asked a single question. Instead, he has put several questions in play, to some of which the answer is 'Yes' and to others the answer is 'No'. This doesn't *always* happen when one asks what someone believes, or answers such a question. Sometimes a sentence "*So-and-so believes that S*" is used to report belief in a single propositional object, whether linguistically enhanced or not. When this is so, it is usually determinate whether the report is true. Even when it is indeterminate which of various propositions is reported believed, the truth value of the report may still be determinate, if the agent believes, or doesn't believe, each proposition about which the report is indeterminate. In such cases the indeterminacy may not matter, even though it is there.

By contrast, Kripke's scenario shows how, in some cases, our normal interpretive practices don't allow us to converge on a single interpretation of an attitude report, but instead make contending interpretations with different truth values available, where the differences among them are relevant to the issues at hand. In such a case, the use of a sentence ⌜Does A believe that S?⌝ will fail to express a determinate or relevantly answerable question because the agent, like Pierre, bears different attitudes to representationally identical but cognitively distinct propositions—while those trying to use ordinary belief ascriptions to report the agent's attitude are unable to pick out objects of the agent's attitudes with sufficient determinacy to yield unique truth values.

MEANING AND UNDERSTANDING

In the section before last, I used the names 'Peter Hempel' and 'Carl Hempel' rather than the philosophically ubiquitous 'Hesperus' and 'Phosphorus', in illustrating linguistic propositions incorporating linguistic modes of presentation. I did so for a reason. Although both pairs of names contribute only referents to propositions semantically expressed by sentences containing them, *understanding* the latter pair requires having information of a sort not required to understand the former. Those well enough informed to employ the names 'Hesperus' and 'Phosphorus' are expected to know that speakers who use them typically presuppose that 'Hesperus' stands for something visible in the evening and 'Phosphorus' stands for something visible in the morning. One who mixed this up would misunderstand, or at the very least not fully understand, the names. Nothing of this sort is true of 'Peter Hempel' and 'Carl Hempel'.

With this in mind, consider an utterance of (12) by a speaker A addressing a hearer B, in a context in which A and B share the presupposition that both understand the names.

12. Hesperus is Phosphorus.

Here, A asserts not only the bare singular proposition expressed by (12), but also the linguistically enhanced proposition entertainable only by those who identify the predication targets via the two names. The cognitive impact of this enhancement is more predictably identifiable and less sensitive to changeable contextual features than are the impacts of similar enhancements involving ordinary names like 'Peter Hempel' and 'Carl Hempel'. Although the enhanced proposition that A asserts merely represents Venus as being identical with Venus, B's entertainment of it puts B in position to draw further conclusions. Knowing that A asserted the linguistically enhanced proposition, and presupposing that A understands the names involved, B reasons that A knows he will be taken to be committed to the claim that *the object Hesperus, visible in the evening sky, is identical with the object Phosphorus, visible in the morning sky*. Realizing that A has done nothing to undermine this expectation, and in fact anticipates this reasoning, B may further conclude, correctly, that A *asserted* the descriptively enriched proposition.

The extra assertive content attached to A's remark arises from (i) the linguistically enhanced proposition A asserted, which incorporates the Millian modes of presentation requiring identification of Venus via the two names, (ii) the shared presupposition that both A and B understand those names, (iii) the descriptive information that comes with such understanding, and (iv) the fact that nothing else about the utterance blocks the reasoning used by B to identify the descriptively enriched assertion. It is important to realize that there are cases in which reasoning of this sort *is* blocked.

Suppose, for example, that the conversation between A and B were to continue as follows:

13a. If Hesperus's orbit had been different it wouldn't appear in the evening. (said by A)

13b. In that case would Hesperus still have been Phosphorus? (asked by B)

13c. Certainly. Hesperus would have been Phosphorus no matter what. (A again)

Here, factors (i)–(iii) remain in place, but (iv) doesn't. Although A's assertive utterance of (13c) commits A to the necessity of the linguistically enhanced proposition that Hesperus is Phosphorus, it *doesn't* commit A to the absurdity that *no matter what the planet's orbit had been*, the unique thing that was both Hesperus and visible in the evening would have been identical with the unique thing that was both Phosphorus and visible in the morning. The difference between the descriptive enrichment of A's use of (12) and the lack of such enrichment of A's use of the modal sentence (13c) hinges on what understanding the names requires. Understanding the names requires knowing that most agents familiar enough to use them take 'Hesperus' to designate something seen in the evening and 'Phosphorus' to designate something seen in the morning.

Presupposing this about each other, A and B assign a rich descriptive content to A's assertive utterance of (12). Since taking the names to designate things *actually* seen at certain times tells one *nothing* about when those things are seen at *possible world-states*, A and B are not tempted to descriptively enrich the modal assertion made by A's use of (13c).

Although nothing could be simpler, the contrast illustrated by (12) and (13c) has been difficult for theorists to accommodate. Some contemporary Millians, fixated on examples like (13c), have mistakenly distrusted descriptive enrichment of assertive content in examples like (12). While followers of Frege have correctly taken the propositions asserted by examples like (12) (in contexts in which the names are understood) to include descriptive contents, they have had trouble with uses of modal examples like (13c). Their trouble comes from misunderstanding the way descriptive information is tied to *understanding* expressions. Many descriptivists have wrongly assumed that the descriptive information needed to understand special names like 'Hesperus' and 'Phosphorus', ordinary names, and natural kind terms are their *semantic contents*. Since they think that all such expressions have semantic contents, they think that the expressions must all have descriptive Fregean senses of one or another sort.

This view is based on three cardinal errors:

(a) the idea that names like 'Hesperus' and 'Phosphorus', which arguably impose substantive descriptive conditions on what it takes to (fully) understand them, are representative of names in general;

(b) the assumption that conditions on (fully) understanding terms—including those like 'Hesperus' and 'Phosphorus'— are incorporated in descriptive senses that determine their referents and are the contributions these terms make to the propositions semantically expressed by (uses of) sentences containing them; and

(c) the presumption that the "cognitive significance" (inference potential) of a proposition p for one who entertains it is exhausted by p's representational content (so representationally identical propositions have the same cognitive significance).

The first idea, (a), is false because there is no standard descriptive information that must be known or believed by those who use most ordinary names; the third idea, (c), is false because, as I have used (12) to illustrate, referentially identical propositions can differ in their inference potential; the second idea, (b), is false because it wrongly incorporates conditions on *understanding* into a term's meaning or semantic content.

Outliers like 'Hesperus' and 'Phosphorus' aside, this final error doesn't show up much in our ordinary talk of names, because we don't normally speak of *what the name 'Saul Kripke'* or *'David Lewis' means*, or of whether one *understands* them. Rather, we are inclined to ask whether one *is familiar* with the names. We are more prone to error with general terms like 'water' and 'heat'. These are directly referential designators of kinds—one a chemical kind involving hydrogen and oxygen, one a physical kind involving motion of molecules. In each case, the kind K is the semantic content that the general term G contributes to propositions semantically expressed by sentences containing G. Given this, plus the idea that the semantic content of G is the meaning of G, one is tempted to think (i) that knowing *what G means* and *understanding G* are the same; (ii) that knowing that K is the meaning of G—which is knowing, of K, that it is the meaning of G—is necessary and sufficient for knowing *what G means*; and (iii) that therefore knowing that K is the meaning G (i.e., knowing, of K, that it is what G means) is necessary and sufficient for understanding G.

This can't be right. To know (the truth of) the proposition expressed by ⌜n is G⌝, where n denotes o, is to know, of K, that o is an instance of it. As Kripke and Putnam taught us, one can know things like this without being able to define what it takes to be an instance of K, or even to reliably identify K's instances. It is enough that there be a general term designating K that one picks up with the intention of preserving the content it has already acquired. It is also enough if one has had limited contact with instances of K, and one uses the term to designate the unique kind (of the relevant type) of which the things one has encountered are instances—where it is tacitly understood that being an instance of a kind involves sharing properties that explain the salient observable characteristics of its instances.[5]

Given all this, one can acquire knowledge of K very easily. One of the easiest things one can come to know is that a certain general term means or stands for K—e.g., that 'water' stands for water and that 'heat' stands for heat. An agent who has acquired these terms by one of the easy routes just mentioned thereby knows, of each relevant K, that the corresponding term G stands for it. But, contrary to (i)—(iii) above, this is *not* sufficient for *understanding* G, let alone for *fully understanding* it in the sense in which we ordinarily speak of such understanding. Such understanding requires more than minimal competence with the term, which is simply the ability to use it to designate what it conventionally designates. *To understand a term is to have the knowledge and recognitional ability to use it to communicate in ways widely presupposed in the linguistic community.*

This dynamic, illustrated using 'Hesperus' and 'Phosphorus', but otherwise rarely found with ordinary names, is nearly always present with natural kind terms. Understanding them—in the sense needed to use them to communicate in ways widely presupposed by

---

[5] See Soames (2007c).

members of one's linguistic community—requires more than knowing of the kinds that the terms designate them. For example, understanding 'water' requires knowing that those who use it standardly presuppose that it stands for something that can take the form of a colorless drinkable liquid, something that falls from the sky in rain, and so on. A similar remark can be made about the general terms 'heat', 'light', and 'red', the (full) understanding of which may require some ability to recognize instances of the designated kinds via the senses, in addition to knowledge of commonplace facts about the kinds and their instances presupposed by most uses of the terms.

Understanding in this sense is *not* a semantic notion in the sense of theories of semantic content. Our ordinary notions of *understanding an expression E* and *knowing what E means* track information commonly presupposed by most speakers who use E—which is only distantly related to the technical notion of *semantic content* or its determinants. For a semantic theory that assigns a given content to E to be correct, most minimally competent speakers must use E with that content, which in turn must typically appear as a constituent of the contents of speech acts performed using E. Widely shared presuppositions about information normally carried by uses of sentences containing E go much further.

These presuppositions together with representationally inert but cognitively significant linguistic modes of presentation pragmatically added to propositions semantically expressed by sentences containing general terms are important for understanding instances of Frege's puzzle like (14).

14a. Water is the substance molecules of which are made up of one hydrogen atom and two oxygen atoms.

14b. Water is H_2O.

14c. Water is water.

The proposition semantically expressed by (14c) predicates identity of the kind water and itself, and so is knowable a priori. The proposition semantically expressed by (14a) is both distinct from proposition (14c) and nontrivial because it involves a genuine description. The status of (14b) depends on whether 'H_2O' is a name or an abbreviated definite description. The most plausible view, I think, is that, like 'Hesperus' and 'Phosphorus', it is a Millian name the understanding of which requires associating it with certain minimal descriptive information. In the case of 'H_2O', the information required to understand it is that it is widely presupposed (and known to be presupposed) by users of the name that it stands for some kind of chemical compound involving hydrogen and oxygen. (Nothing more detailed than that is required for the level of understanding that is most commonly presupposed.) Under these assumptions, (14b) *semantically* expresses the same trivially true proposition that (14c) does. But the pragmatically enhanced proposition that arises from it by requiring the first argument of identity to be identified via the term 'water' and the second to be identified via the term 'H_2O' is new and knowable only a posteriori. Those who believe this proposition, *understanding* both 'water' and 'H_2O', are typically able to infer that assertive uses of (14b) will assert *that the stuff, water, that comes in the form of a colorless, drinkable liquid that falls from the sky in rain, is a chemical compound involving hydrogen and oxygen.* Since speaker-hearers standardly presuppose that they understand the expressions, this highly informative proposition will normally be communicated and even asserted by assertive utterances of (14b).

In this example, *understanding* the terms 'water' and 'H_2O' require having different collateral information about what they stand for, despite the fact that their representational contents are identical. A similar contrast can be drawn in cases in which (fully) understanding one term requires *recognitional ability* not required in order to understand a second term with the same representational content. A case in point is provided by the color term 'red' and what we may take to be a Millian general term 'R' designating the same surface spectral reflectance property that 'red' does.[6] It is plausible to suppose that fully understanding 'red' (in the sense of satisfying what is widely presupposed in contexts in which it is used) requires the ability to visually identify objects that are instances of the color it designates, whereas no such recognitional ability is required to fully understand 'R'.[7] If this is right, then sentences that differ only in the substitution of one of these terms for the other may be used to assert and/or convey different information despite semantically expressing the same proposition. Thus, if I tell you,

15a. The property *being red* just is the property *being R*.

in a context in which it is presupposed that we both (fully) understand 'red' (and so can recognize by sight things to which it correctly applies), then I assert a linguistically enhanced proposition from which, together with background information in the context, you can conclude that various things you visually recognize as being red are also R, despite the fact that you would not be in the position to draw such conclusions had I uttered (15b) or (15c) instead.

15b. The property *being red* just is the property *being red*.
15c. The property *being R* just is the property *being R*.

In cases in which we each know that we both visually recognize certain things to be red, my utterance of (15a) will communicate, and in some cases even assert, that those things are also R.

---

[6] See Soames (2007c) for an analysis of 'red' along these lines.
[7] Since the blind and the color-blind aren't able to do this, they don't count as fully understanding 'red', though they often are able to use it perfectly well to designate its conventional representational content.

Next consider the attitude ascription (16), referring to a monolingual Spanish speaker.

16. Juan has just learned that water is H_2O.

Here, the falsehood semantically expressed by (16) is enriched by requiring one who entertains the object of 'learn' to identify one argument of *identity* via the term 'water' *or some translation of it*, while identifying the other via 'H_2O' *or some translation of it*—T_2 being a translation of T_1 only if conditions for *understanding* them are (roughly) the same. So understood, a use of (16) asserts that Juan has only recently come to believe a certain informative proposition that makes no claims about words or translations. When, as is standard, he is presupposed (i) to understand the relevant terms, and (ii) to take the descriptive information required by such understanding to genuinely apply to the designata of those terms (as, of course, the vast majority of speakers of his language do), the assertive utterance of (16) will result in the assertion and communication of a proposition that characterizes Juan as only recently coming to know *that a certain stuff that comes in the form of a colorless, drinkable liquid and falls from the sky in rain is a chemical compound involving hydrogen and oxygen.*[8] A similar point can be made about uses of (17).

17. Juan has just learned that for any object x whatsoever, it is red iff it is R.

LESSONS FOR FREGE'S PUZZLE AND BEYOND

Like the discussion of earlier examples, this result illustrates how cognitive propositions combined with Millian, and in particular

---

[8] (ii) is essentially the condition that Juan is typical in believing that the *stereotypes* of 'water' and 'H_2O', in the sense of Putnam (1970), are accurate.

linguistic, modes of presentation can be used to great advantage in defusing Frege's puzzle cases involving natural kind terms, attitude ascriptions, and even cases involving ascription of attitudes to agents who speak other languages. The same combination also gives a positive twist to the treatment of the classic example in John Perry (1977) of the amnesiac Rudolf Lingens, trapped in the Stanford University Library reading a fact-filled biography of Lingens that includes a description of his predicament. From his reading, he knows of Rudolf, i.e., *himself*, that he is named 'Rudolf', but doesn't know this *in the first-person way*, and so doesn't self-ascribe being so named. This changes when he remembers "who he is" and *truthfully* says, "*I have just realized my name is 'Rudolf'.*" The truth of his remark requires that the proposition to which he previously did not bear the *realizing* relation be one in which he is identified in the first-person way. This is easily handled by the account given in chapter 3.

Suppose, however, that Rudolf expresses his epiphany using (18a).

18a. I have just realized that I am Rudolf Lingens.

How can his assertion be true? Suppose the library has a mirror. Looking in it, the amnesiac says "I am he," demonstrating RL. In so doing, RL self-ascribes *being RL*, realizing in the first-person way that he is RL. Although this threatens the truth of (18a) on Lewis- or Perry-style analyses, the cognitive analysis of propositions has the resources to avoid the threat. Starting from the semantic content (18b), we first reorganize that content in a form (18c) suitable for representing self-ascription.

18b. Only just now has it been so that: *RL realizes that RL is RL.*
18c. Only just now has it been so that: λx *[x realizes that x = RL] RL.*

Next we proceed with two pragmatic enrichments: one requiring the target of *realizing one is identical with RL* to be identified in the first-person way, and one requiring the second argument of the identity relation to be identified via the name 'Rudolf Lingens'.[9] The larger lesson exhibited by this case is that since all *de se* cases, original or extended, are at bottom variants of Frege's puzzle, they should be treated in similar fashion.

The final lesson to be learned about Frege's puzzle cases from the above discussion of meaning and understanding is that there are two different senses of 'meaning' that must be distinguished. The first sense of meaning is strictly Millian; it is the object or kind that a Millian term stands for. This is what the term contributes to what—in the terminology of contemporary theories of language—is called "the semantic content" of, or "the proposition semantically expressed by," sentences containing it. The second sense of 'meaning' is one in which the meaning of a term—or of a phrase or sentence containing it—is a set of conditions that must be satisfied in order for a speaker to be counted as *understanding* the expression. Sometimes satisfying these conditions requires knowing widely presupposed facts about the semantic content of the expression; sometimes it requires recognitional, verificatory, or inferential abilities concerning that content. The chief error of theories descending from Frege is that they conflate these two kinds of meaning (semantic content vs. that needed for understanding). The chief error of theories descending from Mill is that they have often ignored the second type of meaning. These errors must be corrected if we are to continue to make progress in the study of linguistic meaning and language use. Any adequate theory must recognize the different ways in which the two kinds of meaning contribute to what speakers assert and believe when they use sentences. I have tried, in this chapter, to illustrate how the cognitive conception of propositions fits into this larger picture.

---

[9] Although (18c) serves the purposes of this example, a more complicated representation—*Only just now has it been so that:* λx [x *realizes that* λy ($y = RL$) RL] RL (with two first-person enrichments)—is needed for some cases, including a variant of one discussed in chapter 3.

Perceptual and Demonstrative
Modes of Presentation

ANOTHER MILLIAN MODE OF PRESENTATION:
PERCEPTUAL IDENTIFICATION

Chapters 2–4 introduced several ways of cognitively identifying propositional constituents that can be incorporated into propositions without changing referential content. Notably absent until now has been perception, which is a Millian mode of presentation, or better, a collection of such modes, of the same general sort. One member of the collection is vision, which is itself a vast extended family of this sort. Imagine, to begin with, an agent A watching a bird, B, hop from branch to branch on a tree. Although A visually predicates first one, then another, property of B, A doesn't, while focusing on B, identify B as whatever turns out to uniquely possess this or that property.[1] A's perceptual focus is more direct and immediate. Because of this, there is a cognitive act, and so a proposition, of predicating *being red*, of a predication target B, *that one cognizes visually*. To perform this act, and hence to entertain the

---

[1] Dickie (2010) articulates an account of perceptual acquaintance that brings together experimental literature on psychology with traditional philosophical literature on thought and perception in support of the thesis that the identification of objects in visual perception is direct and conceptually unmediated. Recanati (2010) also defends an account of perceptual acquaintance that distinguishes singular cognition from descriptive cognition.

proposition, requires identifying the target of one's predication visually.

In this example, the property predicated is visually perceivable— one that may itself be a constituent of A's perception. In such a case, A doesn't simply predicate a property of a visually identified object; A's predication of the property occurs in A's visual perception. But this isn't essential. Having identified a perception target perceptually, an agent might predicate a non-perceptual property of it—*being a cardinal, being a type of bird that is rarely found here,* or *being Tom's pet.* In such a case, the agent entertains a perceptually restricted proposition, even though the proposition isn't entertained in perception.

How an object is perceptually identified when one predicates something of it can, of course, affect whether one affirms the predication or judges the resulting proposition to be true. Although B may be Tom's pet cardinal, which he has previously told A about, A may be surprised when you say to A, demonstrating B, "That is Tom's pet cardinal." "Oh," A might respond, *"I didn't realize that it [demonstrating B] was Tom's pet, or even that it was a cardinal."* These assertions appear true, even if A retains his previous knowledge of what Tom told him about B—namely, that B is a cardinal and that B is Tom's pet. For A's *new* assertions to be true, the propositions A claims not to have known must *not* be the bare singular propositions about B that A already knew from Tom's previous testimony. But they may be representationally identical versions of those propositions the entertainment of which requires B to be visually identified.

That these propositions aren't semantically encoded is no objection to the claim that they are asserted, provided one thinks, as I do, that semantic contents of sentences are only starting points for determining what agents assert or otherwise express. Many examples I have discussed in previous chapters have involved pragmatic enrichment of the semantic content of a sentence. For each example S, one

starts with its semantic content and adds, either to it or to a representationally equivalent reorganization of it, restrictions on how one
or more predication targets are cognized. These additions are driven
by the goal of making maximal sense of the speaker's remark. When
no addition is needed, none is made, and the speaker is deemed to
have asserted or expressed the proposition her sentence semantically encodes. When competing additions lead to different assessments of her performance, we select the one that best fits the requirements of the communicative situation. The same reasoning
applies to cases like the one just considered in which restrictions are
added requiring perceptual identifications of predication targets. In
these cases, as with so many others, we deal with sub-cases of Frege's
puzzle by using a new kind of pragmatic enrichment that does not
change representational content.

This is illustrated by a further variation of the story of A's seeing
Tom's pet cardinal B. This time imagine that several days before A's
conversation with you, A *saw* B in Tom's home, judging it then to be
a cardinal, and Tom's pet. A *then* entertained and affirmed the true,
perceptually restricted propositions A fails to affirm when seeing B
later. How, in this version of the story, can we account for the apparent truths A asserts when A responds to your information by uttering
(1a), (1b), or (1c)?

1a. I didn't recognize that bird [demonstrating B] as Tom's pet
    cardinal.
1b. I didn't realize that that bird [demonstrating B] was Tom's
    pet cardinal.
1c. I didn't know that that bird [demonstrating B] was Tom's pet
    cardinal.

All that is required by the truth A asserts in uttering (1a) is that A
didn't, just prior to the report, affirm the proposition p+ that

predicates *being Tom's pet cardinal* of B, the entertainment of which requires one to identify the predication target, B, visually. This is unproblematic, since it means only that A didn't occurrently judge that proposition to be true. Next consider (1b) and (1c). Here, we add that A did, when A saw B earlier in its birdhouse, believe, and perhaps even know, p+.[2] Does A continue to believe or know p+ later, when A refuses to affirm it? Although refusal to affirm a proposition one entertains doesn't prove that one doesn't know or believe it independently, it is plausible to suppose that such refusal *coupled with the lack of a reliable disposition to affirm it* (with appropriate justification) when it is entertained in related circumstances may preclude knowing, or even believing, it. If, in the present case, A isn't very good at recognizing B as Tom's pet cardinal in various perceptual situations, we should suppose that A *doesn't know, and may not even believe,* p+, and hence that the assertions A makes in uttering (1b) and (1c) are true. This is all to the good, since these results seem to be straightforwardly correct.

The case is more complicated when, despite the fact that A nearly always recognizes his wife Mary when he sees her, his failure to do so on a particular occasion leads him to ask, "Is she [demonstrating Mary] my wife? I don't know whether she is or not." How, in this case, can we explain the apparent truth of A's assertion that he doesn't *know* whether she [demonstrating Mary] is his wife? Even though A doesn't, upon seeing her, affirm the pragmatically enriched proposition that she is his wife the entertainment of which requires visually identifying her as predication target, A does retain a robust disposition to affirm that proposition when it is presented to him across a wide range of ordinary circumstances. The fact that A retains

---

[2] More properly, A believed or knew a proposition identical with p+ except for containing a time early than the time t reported on, which A continues to know at t.

this disposition is evidenced by the justice of his companion's rejoin-
der, "You do so know that she [demonstrating Mary] is your wife.
Look more carefully." This suggests that A's original claim to lack
knowledge may be false, and only have appeared true because there
was an evident truth in the vicinity—namely that A didn't, and
couldn't, then *judge* whether she (demonstrating Mary) was his wife,
because A wasn't then in a position to affirm the perceptually enriched proposition that she was. The fact that A could perfectly well
judge, of Mary, *that she was his wife,* and may even then have been
thinking of his good fortune that she was, is accommodated by distinguishing the ordinary singular proposition that predicates *being his
wife* of her from the pragmatically enriched version of it that requires
its predication target, Mary, to be visually identified.

Might we hope for more? Surely, when A failed to recognize
Mary, she was presented to him visually *in some particular way w.*
Indeed, there may be several such *ways,* at different levels of speci-
ficity. Let Pw be a proposition that predicates *being A's wife* of Mary
the entertainment of which requires visually identifying Mary in one
of these specific ways. Presumably, there are such propositions,
which, though entertained by A, were not among those *known* by A.
So far, so good. Still, this doesn't guarantee that A *spoke* truly when
A said to his companion, "I don't know whether she [demonstrating
Mary] is my wife." Although A's audience can identify and entertain
the proposition predicating *being A's wife* of Mary, identified *in some
visual way or other* (which A did know), in certain circumstances A's
companion may *not* be able to identify any more specific visually
enhanced proposition Pw as among those uncertainty about which
prompted A's remark. Since successful assertion requires providing
one's audience a reasonable opportunity of identifying the proposition asserted, circumstances in which A is unable to do this are cases
in which A *didn't assert* or *communicate* that he didn't know Pw. At

best, in such cases, A may have indirectly indicated there to be some proposition he entertained but didn't know in which Mary was identified by him as predication target of *being his wife* by being visually presented to him in some highly specific way.

What assertion or communication of a proposition p requires is not necessarily that hearers be able to entertain p, but that they be able (i) to identify p as something the speaker wishes to assert, and (ii) to determine what is required for p to be true. Think of first-person propositions. When I say "I am in danger" you can entertain one of the propositions I assert—*that SS is in danger*—while identifying and determining what is required for the truth of the representationally identical first-person proposition I also assert. The fact that my utterance makes this information available is what makes it correct to characterize me as asserting both propositions. It is precisely this information that is, or may be, lacking in the case about A and the proposition Pw that predicates *being A's wife of* Mary, the entertainment of which requires Mary to be identified as predication target in the particular, fine-grained visual way w. In that case, A may simply have no very good way of communicating the proposition he entertained but was not able to assess for truth value. If propositions are as I take them to be, there will be many we privately entertain that play important roles in our thought and action, but which we find very difficult, and sometimes impossible, to communicate. Although it is both common and correct to stress the importance of widely sharable propositions, our picture of communication and cognition is not complete without the recognition of less easily sharable propositions of limited accessibility.[3]

---

[3] The limited accessibility of propositions incorporating perceptual modes of presentation is one of two main factors limiting their utility in communication. The other factor is the lack of any clearly exploitable linguistic element—on a par with first-person singular pronouns, temporal indexicals, or the use of the present tense—

So far, most of my examples of such propositions have involved concrete individuals as predication targets. But properties can also be so targeted. Looking at the cardinal, one can focus on its color and predicate properties of it, giving us propositions the entertainment of which requires one to visually identify the color to which one ascribes properties. With this in mind, consider Frank Jackson's famous example of "Black-and-White Mary," a research scientist purported to know all physical truths, despite never having left a black-and-white room (equipped, we may imagine, with black-and-white TV), and so never having seen objects as colored.[4] Since Jackson took physicalism to hold that all truths are physical truths (or a priori consequences of such), he took physicalism to require that every truth must either be known by Mary already or be capable of being derived a priori from those she does know. But surely, since she has never seen anything red, *she doesn't know what red things look like.* Were she to see something red, she would fill this gap in her previous knowledge. But if there is a gap, then physicalism, as Jackson then construed it, is false. This is his famous knowledge objection to (one version of) physicalism.[5]

What is it to know what red things look like? Because of the heavy weather made of this question in the literature provoked by Jackson's example, it can seem difficult to answer. Still, if, on leaving her black-and-white room, Jackson's Mary were to ask us, "What

---

that shows a proposition to be in play that requires those who entertain it to identify a propositional constituent perceptually. Because of this, it is often less clear when a speaker has put such a perceptual proposition in play, and, if the speaker has done so, precisely which one has been put in play. I will return to these issues in chapter 8, where I will assess their broader significance. Until then, I will continue to assume that communication of perceptual propositions is sometimes possible.

[4] Jackson (1982, 1986).

[5] I here put aside the obvious objection that physicalism should not be taken as claiming that all truths are a priori consequences of physical truths. See Soames (2005c), chapters 8 and 9.

do red things look like?," we could give a kind of answer by showing her a comprehensive sample of red objects, and saying, "Red things look like that (or like them)." If we did, she would take herself to have learned something. What she learned is expressible using (2a,b) to predicate the λ-properties given in (2a+,b+) of the property *being red*, when both that property and the objects demonstrated are visually identified.

2a.   For all objects x, if x is red, then x looks like that (or like them, said demonstrating a sample of red objects).

2a+. λP [for all x, if Px, then x looks like $o_1 \ldots o_n$] *Red*

2b.   For all objects x, if redness is the color of x, then x looks like that (or like them, said demonstrating a sample of red objects).

2b+. λz [for all x, if z is the color of x, then x looks like $o_1 \ldots o_n$] *redness*

Being physically omniscient, Mary already knew the ordinary propositions expressed by (2a+) and (2b+). But she didn't know propositions representationally identical to them that require one to *visually identify* the objects as red. After entertaining these propositions, she will retain the disposition to endorse them when they are presented to her, and so know them, *even when not entertaining them.* If our sample objects were well chosen she will also be disposed to endorse *related propositions involving different red things* when the propositions are visually entertained, even though she has not done so up to now.[6] Because of this we can correctly describe her as *knowing what red things look like.* In knowing this, she knows new truths, even though her knowledge of these truths is just her old knowledge plus her new ability to recognize red things by sight. As in other

---

[6] Recall that, by hypothesis, Mary already knew of each red object that it was red.

cases involving Millian modes of presentation, a new way of appre-
hending and affirming a previously known truth counts as knowing
a new truth that is representationally identical to the old one. Since
in Mary's case the new truths are representationally identical to previously known *physical* truths, her previous failure to know these
new truths should not be taken to be a threat to physicalism, which—
without loss to the idea behind Jackson's original characterization
of that doctrine—might now be characterized as the view that all
truths are representationally identical to physical truths. There may
be deeper philosophical issues raised by Jackson's Mary example,
but if so, they involve something beyond the mere fact that Mary
acquires new knowledge.

Visual modes of presentation that don't affect propositional content may also shed light on other well-known philosophical problems. One of these concerns the extent to which it is possible for us
to understand the cognitive and perceptual lives of other, nonhu-
man (even alien) creatures. This is one of the central issues raised
by Thomas Nagel (1974), *"What Is It Like to Be a Bat?"* Since the
perceptual modes of presentation of bats are very different from
ours, it is impossible for us to entertain many of the perceptually
enhanced propositions they do. However, with enough research on
bat perception and bat psychology we may be able to specify representationally identical counterparts of those propositions that
both they and we entertain. With further investigation, we might
even map inferential pathways from their perceptually enriched
propositions to referentially distinct but perceptually neutral propositions available to both species. In this way, it should be possible
in principle to become pretty fully informed about bat psychology
and its relation to ours, despite not knowing what it is like to be a
bat in the sense of being able to entertain many of the propositions
they do.

Visual modes of presentation that don't affect representational content may also provide a new perspective on disputes about qualia and representational theories of mind. Suppose our visual systems could be rewired to make our experience of red things introspectively similar to our previous experience of blue things. If the same could be done for other colors, preserving subjectively discernable relations holding among them, we would vindicate the possibility of spectrum inversion. Since the contents of our perceptual and cognitive experiences (over time) are, I believe, determined by what they are experiences of, it is plausible to suppose that, after a period of adjustment, the *representational* contents of our altered visual experiences and perceptual judgments might be the same as before—with the same properties predicated, in perception and judgment, of the same things. Despite this, we might find our visual experience to be introspectively different than it was before the rewiring. If such a scenario is indeed possible, it must, I think, involve visual modes of presentation, thought of neither as things we perceive, nor as properties things appear to us to have, but as representationally inert but cognitively significant ways we visually identify propositional constituents of propositions the entertainment of which is at least partially perceptual.[7]

DEMONSTRATIVE LANGUAGE AND NON-DEMONSTRATIVE THOUGHT

Although I have discussed several special forms of cognition—first-person, present-tense, linguistic, perceptual, and so on—that, when

---

[7] See Thau (2002) for an insightful discussion of the tension between (i) the genuine attractiveness of the idea that spectrum inversion is possible and (ii) the barriers inherent in attributing that inversion to any difference between the representational contents of agents' perceptual and cognitive experiences before the inversion and the representational contents of their experience afterward.

incorporated in propositions, distinguish them from other, representationally identical, propositions, I haven't made any comparable claim about demonstrative thought or cognition. The reason for this is that I am not convinced there is a special nonlinguistic, *demonstrative way of cognizing* a predication target that isn't one of the perceptual or other Millian modes of presentation already discussed. My skepticism centers on the cognitive significance of what are commonly called "demonstrations." The ordinary sense in which an agent's use of a demonstrative term is accompanied by a demonstration is one in which the agent *does something* to identify *for an audience* some predication target the agent already has in mind. Demonstrations in this sense are not involved in private thought because agents don't determine their cognitive predication targets by demonstrating them to themselves. It is true that some theorists speak of demonstrations in another sense—as things that fix, or determine, the reference of uses of *demonstrative terms*, whatever the fixers may turn out to be. For some theorists, the prime candidates for "demonstrations" in this technical sense are referential intentions. For present purposes, this isn't very useful. Such intentions do not provide a special demonstrative way of cognizing a predication target, whether or not one uses a demonstrative term to refer to it.

The first point to remember is that propositions that don't incorporate linguistic modes of presentation need not involve any linguistic cognition at all. For many propositions, even though entertaining them typically involves focusing one's attention on, or thinking of, one of their constituents, it need not involve *referring* to anything. In these cases there are no referential intentions because reference isn't involved. The next point to notice is that intentions to use a demonstrative term α to refer often involve having o in mind prior to, and independently of, one's use of α. Such cases include those in which one intends to use α to refer to John, whom one presently *perceives*, whom one remembers perceiving, or whom one has singular thoughts about by thinking of him via the name 'John', which one has already acquired. In such cases, the referential intentions to use α to refer to John, sometimes called "demonstrations" by theorists, are *themselves* singular thoughts about John, rather than special ways in which one comes to have singular thoughts about him. In none of these cases is there any distinctively new mode of demonstratively identifying a predication target that is associated with agents' use of demonstrative terms.

The same can be said about cases in which we can name or demonstratively refer to things we have never perceived or even encountered indirectly through a chain of communication with others who have singular thoughts about them. One such case involves my naming or referring to the deer whom I know only through the effects of its regular visits to my garden. In this case and many others our ability to refer to, and have singular thoughts about, things is facilitated by some form of causal contact with those things.[8] However, no simple causal story will do, as is indicated by the fact that, in certain circumstances, we can refer to things we intend to bring into existence, or to certain merely possible things.[9] Some theorists, impressed by these and similar examples, conclude that there is no acquaintance constraint, however loose, on singular thought, and hence that we are capable of having singular thoughts about virtually anything we can uniquely describe.[10] Others, including Saul Kripke, Nathan Salmon, and me, reject such latitudinarianism.[11]

[8] See Salmon (2010) and the penultimate section of Soames (2011) for discussion.

[9] Examples of this sort are presented in Soames (2010a), pp. 128–29. See also Salmon (1987).

[10] Jeshion (2002, 2010b), and Hawthorne and Manley (2012).

[11] Saul Kripke (2011b), Nathan Salmon (2010), Scott Soames (chapter 16 of 2003; chapters 3 and 10 of 2005c).

Fortunately, there is no need to resolve this issue here, since there is nothing in any of the crucial examples or the controversy about them that distinguishes *demonstrative* from *non-demonstrative* direct reference. Hence, I see no case for a special demonstrative form of cognition.

Nevertheless, demonstratives do play a unique and distinctive role in mediating thought and language. Consider uses of simple demonstrative words like 'he' and demonstrative phrases like 'that man wearing a green jacket'.

3a. He is in danger.

3b. That man wearing a green jacket is in danger.

Imagine a case in which I see someone M whom I judge to be a man wearing a green jacket. I perceive M and cognitively predicate being male and wearing a green jacket of him. Assessing the situation further, I come to suspect that M is in danger, which leads me to utter (3a) or (3b). In so doing I use a demonstrative word or phrase to refer to M, while using the predicate 'is in danger' to predicate *being in danger* of M. If it is obvious to my hearers that M is my predication target, no pointing, gesturing, nodding, or other overt demonstration may be needed. In both cases, I am counted as asserting *that M is in danger*.

When using (3a) I am also counted by my audience as thinking of M as male; when using (3b), I am counted as thinking of M as being an adult male and as wearing a green jacket. Thus, I am understood to be committed, in uttering (3a), to M's being both male and in danger, and, in uttering (3b), to M's being both an adult male wearing a green jacket and in danger. But it need be no part of *what I assert* in these cases that M is male, that M is wearing a green jacket, or that I am thinking of him as bearing these properties. These points carry over to uses of (4a,b).

4a. Mary believes he is in danger.

4b. Mary believes that man wearing a green jacket is in danger.

As before, when I assertively utter (4a) or (4b), I am counted as thinking of M as being male, or as being an adult male and wearing a green jacket, as well as asserting that Mary believes that M is in danger. But it is no part of what I assert that Mary believes anything about me or how I think of M, and it need be no part of what I assert that Mary believes that M is male or wearing a green jacket.

In these cases, the determination of the referent of my use of 'he' or 'that man wearing a green jacket' is part and parcel of the determination of what I assert. What is essential to the meanings of these terms, and makes them demonstratives, is that their function is to aid in identifying a referent about which the speaker says or asserts something, often without further contributing to what is said or asserted. A hearer who understands 'he' (or 'that man wearing a green jacket') takes my use of the term to indicate that I believe the individual to be male (or that I believe the individual to be an adult male wearing a green jacket). The hearer also understands that, other than contributing to the determination of the individual being talked about, these (semantic) contributions to reference determination typically *do not* contribute to the representational content of the proposition asserted.

When I speak of "semantic contributions to reference determination," I mean contributions on a par with other factors. The referent of a speaker's use of 'he' in assertively uttering (3a), or 'that man wearing a green jacket' in assertively uttering (3b), is (roughly) the unique individual whom a rational, attentive, and reasonably informed hearer would take the speaker to be asserting to be in danger. If it turns out that the individual M at whom the speaker is staring, and who appears to be threatened by some ominous development, is female, then the speaker will typically have referred to M and said of M that M is in danger, despite also revealing that he or she had wrongly thought that M was male.

Those who speak of "semantic reference" versus "speaker reference" would agree that *the speaker* referred to M, while insisting that *the term the speaker used* failed to have any *semantic reference* in the context. I don't see the point of this addition. When demonstrative terms are involved, there typically is no such thing as the "semantic referent" of the term, or of the proposition "semantically expressed" by the sentence in the context of utterance. The meaning of a demonstrative term seldom, if ever, (alone) determines reference, and the meaning of a sentence containing such a term seldom, if ever, determines a unique proposition. At best there is a referent of the term, and a proposition expressed by the sentence, relative to a particular context. But if contextual information has to be provided, what makes the contextual referent of the term the *semantic* referent, and what makes the contextually expressed proposition one that is *semantically* expressed? I see no way of giving a principled answer. Better, I think, to take the meaning of a demonstrative to be a useful though fallible guide in identifying a referent, and the semantics of a sentence containing it to be a similar guide in identifying the propositional content of the relevant speech act.

In assertively uttering (3a) I assert the bare singular proposition p that predicates *being in danger* of M; in assertively uttering (4a) I assert that Mary believes p. Do I also assert propositions cognitively distinct but representationally identical with these two propositions? Well, I do use the demonstrative pronoun 'he' to identify the predication target of *being in danger*, and, it could be argued, of *being believed by Mary to be in danger*. Since I typically expect my hearer to do the same, I could be counted as asserting, in the case of (3a), the proposition p + that is identical with p except for requiring M to be identified using 'he', and, in the case of (4a), the proposition in which *being believed by Mary to be in danger* is predicated of M by an agent for whom M is presented by a use of 'he'.[12] All of this may be correct, though it is normally not a matter of great significance, since including propositions incorporating these Millian modes of presentation among those asserted by a use of a sentence containing a demonstrative typically doesn't have much effect on the cognitive significance of the discourse.

But there are cases in which it does. Suppose you and I know that M is female, and I tell you that she (M) is in danger. You then ask, "Is Mary aware that she is in danger?," to which I respond, "Well, not exactly, but Mary does believe that *he* is in danger." The analysis of this unusual case may be that the speaker asserted (i) that Mary *doesn't* believe the proposition the entertainment of which requires one to cognize M using the demonstrative pronoun 'she' (or a translation of it) in predicating *being in danger* of M; and (ii) that Mary *does* believe the otherwise identical proposition the entertainment of which requires one to cognize M using the demonstrative pronoun 'he'—thereby conveying, without explicitly asserting, that Mary takes M to be male. The example is, to be sure, a bit awkward, since in giving it, I (the speaker) must use 'he' in reporting Mary's belief to pick out someone you and I both know to be a female. In doing this, I violate the default rule that tells me to use 'he' only to identify a male. But this doesn't cause reference failure, since, in the case imagined, you already know I am referring to M and can see why I am deliberately violating the rule. If this is right, then, sometimes incorporating a Millian mode of presentation involving a demonstrative term δ in the proposition p asserted by an utterance of a

---

[12] Strictly speaking, this last proposition is representationally identical to a proposition that is trivially equivalent (rather than representationally identical) to the proposition that Mary believes p.

sentence containing δ makes a cognitively significant contribution to that assertion (over and above the contribution of the referent of the use of δ to p).

FIRST PERSON, SECOND PERSON, THIRD PERSON

The semantics of demonstratives together with Millian modes of presentation involving them can also help us understand an extension of John Perry's example of the amnesiac Rudolf Lingens trapped in the library reading a story about himself. From his reading, he knows of Rudolf, i.e., *of himself,* that he is named 'Rudolf', but he doesn't know this *in the first-person way,* and so doesn't report his knowledge with a first-person sentence. This changes when he remembers who he is, as we would put it, and *truthfully* exclaims, "I have just realized that my name is 'Rudolf'." As we saw in chapter 4, the explanation of what his epiphany amounts to and of how this claim about what he has just realized can be true depends on the existence of a first-person proposition that only he, Rudolf, can entertain. The extension of the case involves adding another amnesiac, Rudolf's friend Otto, to the story. In the extended case, Otto is reading the same story over Rudolf's shoulder, when he suddenly recovers a portion of *his* memory. This time, however, the recovered memory is not about the agent who is remembering, but someone else. Otto suddenly remembers *Rudolf's* name. When he does, he excitedly utters (5a), which then leads Rudolf to his epiphany.

5a. Your name is 'Rudolf'.

Although Otto's epistemic state before his "second-person epiphany" is comparable to Rudolf's before his "first-person" epiphany, the interaction of the two can be explained without positing a primitive second-person way of cognizing someone being addressed, or any proposition that can be entertained only by an agent who is addressing someone. To know the meaning of (the singular) 'you' is to know that *for x to use it is for x to directly refer to the individual x is addressing* (if there is one). Otto's knowledge of this rule *plus his first-person knowledge that he is using 'you' to address RL* combines with what he suddenly remembers to provide him with *first-person knowledge* that the person, RL, he is addressing is named 'Rudolf', and hence that his assertive utterance of (5a) is true. Otto's remark then allows Rudolf to work out *in a first-person way* that the one, Otto, who just addressed him knows his name. This, in turn, provides Rudolf with *first-person knowledge* that he is named 'Rudolf'. Thus, what might have seemed to call for positing an independent second-person *de se attitude* reduces to the first-person case. In this imagined scenario, Otto has first-person knowledge that in uttering (5a) he is addressing Rudolf, and Rudolf has first-person knowledge that he is the one addressed. Both also know that *what Otto asserts* predicates *being named 'Rudolf'* of the one—RL—being addressed, and so can be true only if that person is named 'Rudolf'. These facts explain the psychologies of Otto and Rudolf, and their interaction.

Nevertheless, there is still a puzzle. Suppose Otto had assertively uttered not (5a) but (5b).

5b. *I've* just realized that *your* name is 'Rudolf'.

There is no problem explaining how this leads Rudolf to his epiphany, or how it was prompted by Otto's new *first-person* belief that RL, whom he is addressing, is named 'Rudolf'. But there is a puzzle about how the attitude ascription Otto asserts in using (5b) could be true. After all, he already knew *de re* of RL that his name was 'Rudolf' from reading the story. He even self-ascribed the property *being one who realizes that RL is named 'Rudolf'*—having been disposed to accept (6a), using 'Rudolf' to name the man he was reading about.

6a. I realize that Rudolf is named 'Rudolf'.

So, if in assertively uttering (5b), Otto asserted either (6b) or (6c), then what he asserted was false.

6b. λx [x is one who only just now has realized that RL is named 'Rudolf'] *I*

6c. Only just now has it been so that [λx [x realizes RL is named 'Rudolf'] *I*]

This seems wrong.

The difficulty we face is that although the first-person epiphany that Otto would express to himself—*"The one, RL, I am addressing is named 'Rudolf'"*—underlies his assertion, it is *not* part of what he asserts. What Otto *asserts* in uttering (5b) is about Rudolf, and what Otto has only just now realized about Rudolf. What he asserts says nothing about his *addressing* anyone, or his only just now realizing the truth of a proposition that represents him as *addressing* someone. Were it not for Millian modes of presentation, this would leave us at an impasse. Without them, representational content would be all there is to a proposition, and Otto's assertion would falsely represent him as only just now realizing that RL is named 'Rudolf'. With Millian modes of presentation, we avoid this incorrect characterization of his remark by taking the proposition asserted to be a double pragmatic enrichment of the bare representational content expressed by (7).

7. Only just now has it been so that [λx [x realizes RL is named 'Rudolf'] Otto]

The first of these enrichments requires the subject, Otto, of the attitude report embedded under the temporal operator to be cognized in the *first-person* way. The second enrichment requires the object of *realizing* to be a certain proposition p that is representationally identical to, but cognitively distinct from, the bare singular proposition that predicates *being named 'Rudolf'* of RL.

We have two choices in identifying this proposition. Both take p to predicate *being named 'Rudolf'* of RL. Entertaining one of those propositions requires RL to be perceptually identified as predication target; entertaining the other requires RL to be identified as predication target by one's use of the second-person singular pronoun. During Otto's time in the library, prior to his epiphany, he did, by virtue of his reading, predicate *being named 'Rudolf'* of RL and affirm that predication, realizing this in the first-person way. But he didn't during that time predicate *being named 'Rudolf'* of anyone presented to him either perceptually or through the use of the second-person singular pronoun (which, of course, he understands). Since he didn't previously do that, he didn't affirm any such predication; nor was he disposed to do so. Because of this, his enlightenment-expressing utterance of (5b) asserted something true and nothing false.

The lesson of this extension of Perry's original puzzle is that although there is what might be called a "second-person way" of cognizing someone, it is *not* on a par with the special first-person way one cognizes oneself. Whereas the first-person Millian mode of presentation is, at bottom, a distinctively nonlinguistic form of cognition, the second-person mode is inherently linguistic. Despite this difference, neither mode is semantically encoded by sentences containing the relevant first- or second-person pronouns. Rather, the assertion and communication of propositions containing these modes is grounded in speaker-hearers' shared knowledge of Kaplan-style semantic rules governing the pronouns, combined with first-person knowledge of when one uses, or is addressed by someone using, the pronouns.

Finally, it should be noted that third-person demonstratives—'he', 'she', etc.—function in very much the same way as second-person demonstratives. Thus, just as we extended Perry's original scenario by introducing Otto and having him converse with Rudolf, so we could extend it again by introducing a third amnesiac, Blotto, with the three protagonists sitting in different parts of the room, reading their own copies of the story. In this extension, Otto has the same epiphany as before, but instead of uttering (5a) or (5b), addressing Rudolf, he utters (8a) or (8b), addressing Blotto, but seen and overheard by Rudolf.

8a. He [pointing at Rudolf] is named 'Rudolf'.

8b. I just realized that he [pointing at Rudolf] is named 'Rudolf'.

Since each of the three characters has first-person knowledge that Otto's use of 'he' designates Rudolf, accepting Otto's remark (8a) amounts to coming to have a new first-person belief, which is the source of Blotto's and Rudolf's epiphanies. The *truth* of Otto's remark (8b) is explained in the same way that the truth of Otto's remark (5b) was in the first extension of the Perry example. In both cases, the content expressed by (7) is enriched with a first-person Millian mode of presentation plus either a perceptual or a demonstrative mode. The only difference is that the demonstrative mode involves the masculine, third-person, singular pronoun rather than the second-person singular pronoun. Either way, the resulting enrichment is both true and cognitively significant. Thus the puzzle is solved.

Recognition of Recurrence

In the preceding chapters I have argued that the cognitive conception of propositions makes room for several different kinds of Millian modes of presentation which, when incorporated in propositions, result in their being representationally identical to, but cognitively distinct from, corresponding propositions lacking them. This chapter raises the question whether another kind of cognition— called cognizing *as the same* in Kit Fine (2007) and *recognizing recurrence* in Salmon (2012)—is a Millian mode of presentation. This form of cognition is a matter of how an agent's identification of an item x at one moment is related to the agent's identification of x at another moment. It is not a matter of predicating identity of the pair consisting of an item x cognized earlier and that same item x cognized now. Rather it is a kind of merging of the representational contents of the two cognitions. When one has cognized x before, in predicating *being F* of x, and one now *recognizes x recurring* as predication target of *being G*, one is in a position to predicate *being both F and G* of x without appeal to further premises. When one doesn't recognize x as recurring, this isn't so. Even if one did cognize x before and now, when cognizing x again, one *suspects* that the items cognized are identical—or *believes*, by virtue of weighing the evidence, that they are—one does not, thereby, *recognize* x as recurring. To recognize recurrence is to immediately and noninferentially connect the information carried by one cognition with information carried by one or more other cognitions.

Recognition of this kind can occur in, and across, different cognitive modalities. Just as one can recognize x through different perceptions of x, so one can recognize x first by being presented with x visually and then by being presented with x cognitively, in either linguistic or nonlinguistic thought. One may recognize x recurring through different linguistic presentations either by recognizing recurrences of a single expression that presents x, or by recognizing occurrences of cognitively equivalent expressions that do so. Either way, a single content is recognized as recurring.

My present task is to determine how, if at all, *recognition of recurrence* fits into the cognitive conception of propositions. In doing so I will draw on earlier discussions of Fine and Salmon, who, despite their contrasting views, have both broken new ground. The crucial questions are (i) whether *recognition of recurrence* is a Millian mode of presentation that distinguishes propositions incorporating it from their representationally identical counterparts, and (ii) whether, if it is, propositions incorporating it are meanings of some sentences. Fine answers 'yes' to both questions, and takes his answer to provide a semantic solution to Frege's puzzle. Salmon answers 'no' to the first question, which renders the second moot. For him solving Frege's puzzle doesn't involve recognizing pairs of cognitively distinct but representationally identical propositions.

Though I disagree with Salmon about the role of cognitively distinct but representationally identical propositions in dealing with some instances of Frege's puzzle, my understanding of *recognition of recurrence* and its significance for semantics, and for Frege's puzzle, is closer to Salmon's than to Fine's. While I accept Fine's idea that there are pairs of representationally identical propositions that differ only in that entertaining one, but not the other, requires the agent to recognize recurrences of a propositional constituent, I think it is more difficult to show that such propositions play leading roles in resolving instances of Frege's puzzle than he does. Moreover, I don't take recognition of recurrence to play *any* role in the *semantics* of sentences containing multiple occurrences of the same, or synonymous, expressions. Thus, I don't think that propositions semantically expressed by these sentences ever incorporate *recognition of recurrence* as a Millian mode of presentation.

Nor do I believe that the inferential significance of recognition of recurrence in discourses in which the same expression recurs in different sentences justifies Fine's contention that whole discourses, rather than individual sentences, are the proper units of a theory of linguistic meaning. Rather, I agree with Salmon's slogan "No cognition without recognition," which is a short (and only slightly exaggerated) way of putting the idea that *recognition of recurrence* is ubiquitous in virtually all our reasoning from one set of propositions to another.[1] Although typically irrelevant to the consequence relation between premises and conclusions, it is routinely required in order for agents to *recognize* instances of that relation, and to *infer* specific conclusions from particular premises. The very pervasiveness of recognition strongly suggests that it isn't a semantic feature of expressions arising from specific linguistic conventions, but a pragmatic feature of thought that agents bring to all their experience, linguistic and nonlinguistic alike.[2]

In this chapter I begin by granting, for the sake of argument, a key idea: that *recognition of recurrence* can function as a Millian mode of presentation. I next argue that even if there are propositions incorporating such modes, they aren't *semantically* expressed by

---

[1] Salmon (2012), 427.
[2] See section 3 of Salmon (2012) for extensive discussion.

sentences. I will then revisit the question of whether there are *RR-requiring propositions* that can be entertained only by those who recognize the recurrence of their constituents. Since propositions are purely representational acts that can incorporate cognitively significant ways of identifying their constituents, it is natural to think that there are. As we shall see, however, the issue is not simple.

THE EFFECT OF RECOGNITION OF RECURRENCE ON ASSERTION AND INFERENCE

Much of the discussion in Fine (2007) is focused on recognizing different occurrences of expressions as presenting a single content. As Fine stresses, such recognition comes in two varieties: (i) recognizing recurrences of a single expression presenting a single content, and (ii) recognizing a single content recurring through presentations of different expressions (e.g., an anaphoric occurrence of a pronoun and its antecedent). In both cases, one content is recognized as recurring throughout different presentations. This, Fine thinks, is reflected in the assertive content of both individual sentences and larger discourses. Starting with individual sentences, he assumes that typical assertive utterances of (a) and (b) in (1) and (2) result in the assertion of different propositions—despite the fact that they represent the same properties and relations being instantiated by the same things.

1a. Carl Hempel bears R to Carl Hempel.
1b. Peter Hempel bears R to Carl Hempel.
2a. Carl Hempel is F and Carl Hempel is G.
2b. Carl Hempel is F and Peter Hempel is G.

Although the (a) and (b) propositions predicate the same n-place properties of the same things, the proposition asserted by a typical utterance of (a), but not the proposition asserted by an utterance

(b), is said to be *coordinated*, requiring one who entertains it to recognize Mr. Hempel as recurring in different argument places.

This point of departure is plausible. There certainly is such a
thing as *recognizing* an item recurring through a sequence of presentations. This can happen in perception and nonlinguistic thought,
when one predicates a property of something one glances at or
thinks about, and follows up with further cognitive acts of the same
sort. In such cases, one's recognition of the predication targets of
various properties is linked; the targets are recognized as recurring
without an accompanying identity predication. A single object can
also be recognized through a series of linguistic presentations—
sometimes by what are themselves *recognized recurrences* of the same
name or other expression and sometimes by occurrences of different
but related expressions. Because of this, the cognitive act of using
(1a) to predicate R of Mr. Hempel and Mr. Hempel, or the act of
using (2a) to predicate F of him and G of him, may differ cognitively
from similar predications using (1b) and (2b). Although in both the
(a) and the (b) cases, we identify the same arguments of the same
properties or relations, typically when using (a) our identification of
them involves *recognizing Mr. Hempel's recurrence*. Though such recognition *can* occur when using (b), it is far less likely to do so.

There are, in principle, two ways of accounting for the different
assertive and communicative contents of uses of these (a) and (b)
sentences. On one (traditional) story, the speaker's use of (1a) asserts the bare singular proposition that predicates R of Mr. Hempel
and Mr. Hempel. Recognizing the recurrence, speaker-hearers trivially infer *that $\lambda x (xRx)$ Mr. Hempel*, which is a separate proposition
that also counts as asserted. The treatment of (2a) is similar; the
proposition *that $\lambda x (Fx \& Gx)$ Mr. Hempel* is asserted as an obvious
consequence of what is explicitly asserted. Utterances of (1b) and
(2b) that don't involve recognition of recurrence don't result in these

extra assertions because without recognition the inferences needed to reach them are not cognitively accessible.

Fine's account—which builds *recognition of recurrence* into one of the propositions asserted by uses of the (a) sentences and *nonrecognition* into one of the propositions asserted by uses of the (b) sentences—is different. The cognitive conception of propositions accommodates this by distinguishing three distinct but representationally identical propositions corresponding to (1a) and (1b).

P1ab. The act of predicating R of Mr. Hempel and Mr. Hempel (however the arguments are identified), *whether or not one recognizes Mr. Hempel's recurrence.*

P1a. The act of predicating R of a pair of arguments, Mr. Hempel and Mr. Hempel, *identifying him in a way that involves recognizing his recurrence.*

P1b. The act of predicating R of a pair of arguments, Mr. Hempel and Mr. Hempel, *identifying him without recognizing his recurrence.*

Whereas one who assertively utters (1b) may assert and communicate P1b, one who assertively utters (1a) typically asserts and communicates P1a. P1ab is also asserted and communicated in both cases. One who accepts P1a is immediately in a position to draw a conclusion, expressed by (1c), that could not immediately be drawn from P1ab or Pb.

1c. Someone, namely Mr. Hempel, bears R to himself—i.e., λx *(xRx) Mr. Hempel.*

Analogous remarks can be made about sentences (2a,b), propositions P2ab, P2a, and P2b, and the immediate inference to (2c) that comes from accepting P2a.

P2ab. The act of conjoining a pair of propositions one of which is the act of predicating F of Mr. Hempel (however identified) and one of which is the act of predicating G of Mr. Hempel (however identified), *whether or not one recognizes his recurrence.*

P2a. The act of conjoining a pair of propositions one of which is the act of predicating F of Mr. Hempel and one of which is the act of predicating G of Mr. Hempel, where *one recognizes Mr. Hempel recurring* when one identifies him as argument of F and of G.

P2b. The act of conjoining a pair of propositions one of which is the act of predicating F of Mr. Hempel and one of which is the act of predicating G of Mr. Hempel, where *one doesn't recognize Mr. Hempel as recurring* when one identifies him as argument of F and of G.

2c. Someone, namely Mr. Hempel, is both F and G—i.e., λx *(Fx & Gx) Mr. Hempel.*

As in other cases, representationally identical propositions can differ cognitively in a way that allows an agent who entertains one to extract further information by inference that is not immediately available to an agent who entertains the other.

It is crucial to notice, however, that the inference-enhancing power of the recognition of recurrence is not limited to operating within the cognition of individual sentences or propositions. Nearly all inference from premises to conclusions requires such recognition across sentences or propositions. Thus, the cognitive phenomenon that occurs within the use of a single sentence, or within a complex cognitive act that is the entertainment of a single proposition, equally occurs across the use of many sentences, or across a connected sequence of cognitive events in which one entertains many propositions. Just as one who recognizes the recurrence of content associated with a use of sentence (2a) is able to immediately infer (2c)—which remains cognitively inaccessible to one who fails to recognize the recurrence when (2b) is used—so one who recognizes the recurrence in (3a) can infer (3c), which one who fails to recognize the recurrence cannot.

3a. Carl Hempel was a famous philosopher. . . . When he taught at Princeton, he lived on Lake Lane. . . . Carl was an early riser who used to compete with Paul Benacerraf to be first to arrive at work in the morning.

3b. Carl Hempel was a famous philosopher. . . . When he taught at Princeton, he lived on Lake Lane. . . . Peter was an early riser who used to compete with Paul Benacerraf to be first to arrive at work in the morning.

3c. Carl Hempel was an early-rising philosopher who taught at Princeton and lived on Lake Lane.

This example illustrates that inferentially significant cognitive recognition is not limited to individual sentences or propositions, but is ubiquitous whenever inferences are drawn. It also shows that recognition is not limited to cases in which the same content is presented by multiple occurrences of the same expression. Since 'Carl Hempel', 'Carl', and 'he' are distinct expressions, the recognized recurrence in (3a) is a recurrence not of terms, but of content. Although the same might true of (3b) for some intimates of Mr. Hempel who freely and automatically interchange 'Peter' and 'Carl' in referring to him, it is not true for most of us. For most of us, getting from (3b) to (3c) requires the information that comes from being told "Peter Hempel is Carl Hempel."

What "information" is that? It's not *that Mr. Hempel is Mr. Hempel*; nor is it *that 'Carl Hempel' and 'Peter Hempel' are coreferential*. We do, of course, obtain that metalinguistic information by accepting (4).

    4.   Peter Hempel is Carl Hempel.

But the metalinguistic information doesn't function as a *premise* in getting from (3b) and (4) to (3c). In such cases, our reasoning is done *in language*, without being *about language*.

When we accept (4), we affirm a proposition that predicates identity of the pair Mr. Hempel, cognized via the name 'Peter Hempel', and Mr. Hempel, cognized via the name 'Carl Hempel'. Inferring proposition (3c) from this plus (3b) depends on *recognizing* Mr. Hempel recurring as the target of different predications in the propositions we use (3b), (4), and (3c) to entertain. Implicitly recognizing recurrences of 'Carl Hempel' in (3b), (4), and (3c), and taking 'he' in (3b) to be linked to the name, we recognize the single recurring content, Mr. Hempel, as predication target of *being a famous philosopher* . . . (in discourse 3b), as predication target of *being one who taught at Princeton* and *being one who lived on Lake Lane* . . . (in 3b), as predication target of *being an early-rising philosopher who* . . . (in proposition 3c), and as one of the two predication targets of identity (in 4). Treating 'Peter' occurring in (3b) as a variant of 'Peter Hempel' in (4), we recognize Mr. Hempel, recurring as predication target of *being an early riser* . . . (in 3b) and as one of the two predication targets of identity (in 4). The cognitive effect of the identity predication in (4) allows us to unite elements of the two streams of recognition—one involving cognitions of Mr. Hempel via the name 'Carl Hempel' and other expressions linked to it, and one involving cognitions of 'Peter Hempel' and expressions linked to it. Thus, we are able to infer (3c) from (3b) and (4).

Although this reasoning is linguistically mediated, it is always about Mr. Hempel, and never about expressions referring to him. We do, of course, perceive and use the expressions, but we don't entertain, affirm, or reject propositions about them. In using them to entertain propositions about their referents, we *recognize* some of the expressions as *recurring*, but only in the sense of treating occurrences of them as uses of the same cognitive tool.

SEMANTICS VS. PRAGMATICS

What, if anything, does recognition of recurrence have to do with semantics? Fine takes it to be central. He takes sentences (1a) and (1b) to differ in meaning because, he thinks, understanding (1a) requires recognizing recurrences of the name 'Carl Hempel' in the sentence and recurrences of the man Carl Hempel in the proposition expressed, while understanding (1b) doesn't require such recognition. On this picture, the propositions semantically expressed by the two sentences both predicate R of < Mr. Hempel, Mr. Hempel >, while predicating nothing further of anything else. But whereas the proposition expressed by (1a) requires one who entertains it to recognize Mr. Hempel recurring as first and second argument of R, the proposition expressed by (1b) does not.

The same idea leads Fine to advocate a theory that assigns sequences of propositions as linguistic meanings of entire discourses, where two such sequences can differ solely in that one can be entertained only by those that recognize certain recurrences of their common elements, while the other does not. I contest this. For me, recognition is a ubiquitous feature of thought and inference, and hence not an essentially linguistic matter at all. When language enters the picture, some cognition becomes linguistic, which means that recognition of recurrence of the same word or expression often serves as a way of recognizing recurrence of the same thought content. But this doesn't have anything to do with semantics.

The point is nicely illustrated by an example from Kripke (1979), involving his character, Peter, who knows Paderewski to be a statesman he discusses with his political friends, while also knowing Paderewski to be a musician he discusses with his musical friends. In both cases, Peter uses 'Paderewski', the name of the famous statesman-musician. For a long time it doesn't occur to Peter that he might be using the name on different occasions to refer to the same man. During this period, he doesn't *recognize* the name *recurring* in his speech, or the man *recurring* in his thoughts; he mistakenly thinks that he is using different names for different men. At some point, however, he has doubts and uses (5a) to ask a pertinent question.[3]

> 5a. Is Paderewski the musician the same man as Paderewski the statesman?

In asking this question, Peter uses the same name twice to present the same content without recognizing any recurrence, of name or content. Although this is a kind of ignorance or error, it is the kind that can crop up in unexpected circumstances, to which no amount of language learning can render one immune. Peter *understands* the sentence he utters; he doesn't misunderstand or misuse it to ask a defective or incoherent question—which he would, if the proposition *semantically* expressed by

> 5b. Paderewski the musician is the same man as Paderewski the statesman.

---

[3] Here I extend Kripke's example slightly by having Peter ask the above question.

required recognizing the recurrence of Paderewski in order to be entertained.

For this reason, I take the linguistic meanings of, and hence the propositions semantically expressed by, (6a) and (6b) to be the same.

6a. The famous philosopher, Carl Hempel, is the same man as the elderly gentleman, Carl Hempel, to whom you were just introduced.

6b. The famous philosopher, Carl Hempel, is the same man as the elderly gentleman, Peter Hempel, to whom you were just introduced.

Although recognition of Mr. Hempel's recurrence is much more natural for a use of (6a) than for (6b), it is hardly inevitable—since the point of uttering (6a) might be to inform one's hearer that she is not in a position like Peter's in the Paderewski case. Moreover, there is nothing special about the fact that the examples in (5) and (6) involve an identity claim, as opposed to some other relational statement. Someone wondering about the relationship between the famous philosopher Carl Hempel and the elderly gentleman Carl Hempel, to whom one had been introduced, might use (6c) to express a suggestive similarity without *recognizing* Mr. Hempel's recurrence in the proposition asserted, let alone *asserting* a proposition the entertainment of which required one to recognize his recurrence.

6c. The elderly gentleman, Carl Hempel, to whom you were just introduced seems to have many of the same friends as the famous philosopher, Carl Hempel.

But if recurrence of the same univocal name in sentences used by speakers who understand them isn't sufficient to guarantee recognition of recurring content in the propositions asserted, then surely the propositions *semantically expressed* by such sentences don't require recognition of recurrence in order to be entertained.

Next consider a use of (7) in which 'Carl Hempel' and 'Carl' are used to refer to Mr. Hempel.

7. Carl Hempel published *Aspects of Scientific Explanation* in 1965, which was ten years after Carl joined the Princeton department.

If there are propositions the entertainment of which require one to recognize recurring constituents, it is plausible to suppose that (7) could be used to assert or otherwise communicate one of them. Presumably, this could be a feature of the meaning of (7) only if the expressions 'Carl Hempel' and 'Carl' here used are really mere variants of the same name. But then surely 'ketchup' and 'catsup' are also variants of the same term, in which case Salmon's example of the ability of someone who understands (8) to use it to ask a perfectly cogent question is further demonstration that recurrence of a term does not semantically require recognition of recurrence of its content in propositions semantically expressed by sentences containing multiple occurrences of the term.[4]

8. Is catsup ketchup?

To sum up, it is not part of the meaning of a sentence containing two occurrences of the same term that a competent speaker capable of using it to designate its conventional content will always be able to *recognize* recurrences of the term, let alone that such an agent will always be able to *recognize* recurrences of the content presented by uses of it. The case is similar for pairs of distinct but synonymous expressions like 'doctor' and 'physician'. Often those

---

[4] Nathan Salmon (1989a, 1990).

who understand both will know *that they have the same content*, and may even *recognize* the common content recurring through presentations first by one member of the pair and then by the other. But such recognition is not part of the meanings of sentences containing the terms. On the contrary, it is possible to understand both terms well enough to use them to express their common content without knowing *that they have the same content*, or *recognizing* recurrences of that content in propositions expressed by sentences one understands that contain the expressions.[5]

Further indication that recognition of recurrence of propositional constituents is *not* semantically encoded in sentences is provided by (9).

9. John fooled Mary into believing that he, John, wasn't John.

Typically, a speaker who uses (9) will recognize John recurring in the proposition expressed, while expecting and even knowing that his audience will too. But it would be absurd to ascribe to Mary belief in a proposition from which it could trivially be inferred *that John is non-self-identical*. Rather, the proposition she is reported, i.e., asserted, to believe is the negation of the proposition that predicates identity of John and John, *with no requirement that one who entertains it recognize John's recurrence*. If the propositions semantically encoded by sentences containing recurrences of the same name required that those who entertained, or bore other attitudes to, them to recognize recurrences of the content of the name, this would not be so. On the contrary, the semantic content of the complement of

---

[5] See Stephen Reiber (1992). In cases like 'doctor' and 'physician' one may understand that both designate professionals whose career is to tend the sick, in cases like 'catsup' and 'ketchup' one may understand that both designate popular tomato-based condiments, and in cases like 'dwelling' and 'abode' one may know that both are residences of some sort.

'believe' would require such recognition, and the proposition semantically expressed by (9) would be transparently absurd. The fact
that it isn't absurd indicates that such recognition is *not* semantically
required.

Another example pointing to this conclusion involves the use of
indexicals. Here we imagine Venus overhearing Mary sincerely
utter (10a).

> 10a. That [pointing to a picture taken of Venus in the morning]
> is visible only in the morning and that [pointing to a picture
> of Venus taken in the evening] is visible only in the evening.
> (said by Mary)

On hearing this, Venus could truly report Mary's assertion and belief
to her audience, Mercury and Mars, using (10b).

> 10b. Mary said and believed that I am visible only in the morning
> and I am visible only in the evening. (reported by Venus)

But Venus could *not* correctly go on to use (10c).

> 10c. Mary said and believed that something—namely me—has
> the property of being *both visible only in the morning and vis-*
> *ible only in the evening.*

If the *semantic content* of the complement of the attitude verbs in
(10b), relative to Venus's context of utterance, *encoded* the requirement that the recurrence of Venus be recognized by one who entertained the proposition, then the *semantic content* of (10b) would be
one from which (10c) could transparently be inferred, and so would
wrongly characterize Mary as believing an obvious absurdity. Since
Venus's use of (10b) doesn't guarantee that inference to be truth-
preserving, there is no such semantic encoding. This is so despite the
fact that Venus correctly expects Mars and Jupiter to recognize the

recurrence in the content of her report—and so to infer that what Mary is reported to have asserted and believed couldn't possibly be true. Crucially, they do *not* take Venus to attribute to Mary belief in a proposition the absurdity of which would be evident to anyone who entertained it—as would anyone who recognized Venus's recurrence.[6]

FREGE'S PUZZLE AND RECOGNITION OF RECURRENCE

Although propositions the entertainment of which requires *recognition of recurrence* are not semantically encoded, the availability of such propositions as assertive and communicative contents of utterances *might* still allow us to resolve some instances of Frege's puzzle pragmatically that would otherwise be difficult to accommodate. A *prima facie* case that it would is provided by Kripke's character Peter. Prior to his enlightenment about the name 'Paderewski' and its bearer, Peter's acceptance, or assertive utterance, of (11a) didn't prompt him to affirm the proposition expressed by (11b), despite the fact that his acceptance or assertive utterance involved affirming a proposition containing recurrences of Paderewski.

11a. . . . Paderewski . . . Paderewski . . .

11b. $\lambda x[. . . x . . . x . . .]$ Paderewski

---

[6] See Soames (2012) for an explanation of why examples along the lines of (9) and (10) cannot be handled by (i) taking recognition of recurrence to be semantically encoded, but (ii) treating attitude ascriptions as systematically ambiguous, having one reading that ignores requirements of recognition of recurrence in their complement clauses and another reading that does not. This won't work because variants of (9), (10), and similar examples can be constructed in which the recurrence of certain elements must be recognized while the recurrence of other elements need or must not be. These examples suggest that requirements that recurrence be recognized are never semantically encoded, but, at best, may be added opportunistically to any or all recurring elements as demanded by the presuppositions of speaker-hearers in contexts of utterance.

The same can be said about Peter's use of (12a) and (12b) in cases in which he presupposes Mary to share his epistemic perspective.

12a. Mary believes that . . . Paderewski . . . Paderewski . . .

12b. Mary believes that $\lambda x[. . . x . . . x . . .]$ Paderewski

After Peter's enlightenment, his acceptance or assertive utterance of (11a) will license accepting (11b), while his acceptance or assertive utterance of (12a) in a situation in which Mary is presupposed to share his enlightenment will license accepting (12b). It might be argued that this difference is best explained by taking the propositions Peter accepts or asserts in using (11a) and (12a) before and after his enlightenment to differ in that the post-enlightenment propositions can be entertained only by one who recognizes Paderewski's recurrence.

But is that explanation superior to competing explanations? Consider again examples (1a,b) and (2a,b).

1a. Carl Hempel bears R to Carl Hempel.

1b. Peter Hempel bears R to Carl Hempel.

2a. Carl Hempel is F and Carl Hempel is G.

2b. Carl Hempel is F and Peter Hempel is G.

Typically, one who assertively utters (1a) or (2a) will be taken to be committed to the propositions expressed by (1c) or (2c), and, since one is normally taken to assert obvious consequences of things one explicitly asserts, one will also be taken to have asserted those propositions.

1c. Someone, namely Mr. Hempel, bears R to himself.

2c. Someone, namely Mr. Hempel, is both F and G.

This is not true of typical utterances of (1b) or (2b). One possible explanation of this holds that utterances of (1a) and (2a) result in

assertions of propositions P1a and P2a, which are pragmatic enrichments of the semantic contents, P1ab and P2ab, of (1a) and (2a)
(which are also asserted).

P1ab. The act of predicating R of Mr. Hempel and Mr. Hempel
       (however the arguments are identified), *whether or not one
       recognizes his recurrence.*

P1a.   The act of predicating R of a pair of arguments, Mr. Hem-
       pel and Mr. Hempel, *identifying him in a way that involves
       recognizing his recurrence.*

P1b.   The act of predicating R of a pair of arguments, Mr. Hem-
       pel and Mr. Hempel, *identifying him without recognizing his
       recurrence.*

P2ab. The act of conjoining a pair of propositions one of which
       is the act of predicating F of Mr. Hempel (however identi-
       fied) and one of which is the act of predicating G of Mr.
       Hempel (however identified), *whether or not one recognizes
       his recurrence.*

P2a.   The act of conjoining a pair of propositions one of which
       is the act of predicating F of Mr. Hempel and one of which
       is the act of predicating G of Mr. Hempel, where *one recog-
       nizes him as recurring* when one identifies him as argument
       of F and of G.

P2b.   The act of conjoining a pair of propositions one of which
       is the act of predicating F of Mr. Hempel and one of which
       is the act of predicating G of Mr. Hempel, where *one doesn't
       recognize him as recurring* when one identifies him as argu-
       ment of F and of G.

Although P1a is representationally identical to P1ab and P2a is representationally identical to P2ab, the pairs differ in their potential
informativeness. One who asserts or affirms P1a (and thereby P1ab

too) by uttering or accepting (1a) *recognizes* the recurrence of Mr. Hempel, and so is able to trivially deduce proposition (1c), which is also asserted. The story is the same for (2a), P2a, and (2c). By contrast, one who utters or accepts (1b) or (2b) typically asserts or affirms P1b or P2b (and thereby P1ab or P2ab) without licensing any inference to (1c) or (2c). On this account, the cognitive difference between accepting or uttering sentences that differ only in codesignative Millian names is explained by incorporating *recognition of recurrence* as a mode of presentation into the propositions affirmed or asserted in one case but not the other.

Although this explanation runs smoothly, an equally smooth explanation involving *recognition of recurrence* is available that doesn't incorporate such recognition into any proposition. If (1a) or (2a) is uttered in a context in which all parties recognize 'Carl Hempel' as recurring, then all parties will recognize Mr. Hempel's recurrence in the bare singular proposition semantically expressed by the sentence and asserted by one's utterance of it. Because of this, the proposition expressed by (1c) or (2c) will be a consequence of what is asserted that is cognitively accessible to speaker-hearers, and so will itself count as asserted. Since we don't get these results with standard utterances of (1b) and (2b), we can explain the cognitive and assertive difference between accepting or uttering the (a) sentences versus accepting or uttering the (b) sentences, whether or not *recognition of recurrence* is incorporated as a Millian mode of presentation into any propositions asserted or believed in these cases.

If Frege's puzzle cases require *recognition of recurrence* to be treated as a Millian mode of presentation, the examples must involve attitude ascriptions. Even so, the case for incorporating such modes in individual propositions is more difficult to make than one might expect.

13a. Mary asserted/believed that Carl Hempel bears R to Carl Hempel.

13b. Mary asserted/believed that Peter Hempel bears R to Carl Hempel.

13c. Mary asserted/believed that someone, namely Mr. Hempel, bears R to himself.

14a. Mary asserted/believed that Carl Hempel is F and Carl Hempel is G.

14b. Mary asserted/believed that Peter Hempel is F and Carl Hempel is G.

14c. Mary asserted/believed that someone, namely Mr. Hempel, is both F and G.

Although the (a) ascriptions semantically express the same propositions as the (b) ascriptions, which may be among the propositions asserted by utterances of the (a) ascriptions, such utterances often result in the assertion of other propositions, too. In many contexts in which (a) is used, speaker-hearers' joint recognition of recurrence of the name 'Carl Hempel' in the sentence and of the man Carl Hempel in the proposition expressed, may, unless the speaker indicates otherwise, result in a default presupposition that Mary, too, recognizes the recurrence in the proposition she is reported to assert or believe. As a result, it may be argued that assertive utterances of (a) often assert and/or communicate (c), while assertive utterances of (b) typically do not. This reasoning will go through, whether or not we incorporate *recognition of recurrence* of Mr. Hempel into any proposition Mary is explicitly reported to have asserted or believed.

A better case for including *recognition of recurrence* in some propositions may result from imagining a post-enlightenment version of Kripke's Peter assertively uttering (15a) or (15b).

15a. I only recently realized (what everyone else realized all along) *that it is true both that Paderewski is a musician and that Paderewski is a statesman.*

15b. I only recently realized (what everyone else realized all along) *that the proposition that Paderewski is a musician and the proposition that Paderewski is a statesman are both true.*

If, as one may plausibly suppose, Peter could use these sentences to assert truths (without asserting falsehoods), then the propositions the complement clauses contribute to those assertions can't be their semantic contents, which predicate joint truth of a pair of bare singular propositions (since Peter affirmed those predications all along).[7] These newly recognized truths *could be* propositions structurally and referentially identical to the semantic contents of the complement clauses of (15a,b), but differing from them in requiring one who entertains them to recognize the recurrence of Paderewski in the constituent propositions.

Could they be anything else? Could they be those expressed by the complements of (16a,b,c)?

16a. I only recently realized (what everyone else realized all along) *that λx (it is true that x is a musician and x is a statesman) Paderewski*—i.e., that Paderewski is such that it is true that he is both a musician and a statesman.

16b. I only recently realized (what everyone else realized all along) *that λx (it is true that x is a musician and it is true that x is a statesman) Paderewski*—i.e., that Paderewski is such that the propositions that he is a musician and that he is a statesman are both true.

---

[7] Recall that, on the view I have defended in previous chapters, semantic contents are only starting points for determining what is asserted, and often end up not being asserted themselves.

16c. I only recently realized (what everyone else realized all
along) λx *(x is a musician and x is a statesman) Paderewski*—
i.e., that Paderewski is both a musician and a statesman.

Although taking the assertions made by uses of (15) to be represented by (16) would account for their truth, one might feel uneasy
about the structural divergence of the complements of (15) from the
semantic contents of the complements of (16). When choosing between competing accounts of assertive pragmatic enrichment, it is
not a bad principle to choose the one that adheres most closely to
the structure of the content being enriched.

Perhaps this argument can be strengthened by adding some complexity to the example. Consider an assertive utterance of (17a) in a
context in which one recognizes all recurrences of the names in the
sentence uttered and all recurrences of their contents in the proposition asserted.

17a. aRba & bRbc & cRba

Among the propositions one is then in a position to infer will be
those expressed by (17b–i).

17b. λx (xRbx) a
17c. λx (xRxc) b
17d. cRba
17e. λx (xRbx & cRbx) a
17f. λx (aRxa & xRxc) b
17g. λx (bRbx & xRba) c
17h. λx (xRxc & cRxa) b
17i. λx (aRxa & xRxc & cRxa) b

Although all of these are cognitively accessible consequences of what
is asserted, there is probably too much complexity to take each of

them, or their conjunction, to be asserted—as opposed to being propositions inferable from what is asserted. What about (18a), which is rendered in English as (18b)? This proposition, it might be argued, is too complex and structurally different from the semantic content of (16a) to count as the proposition asserted by an utterance of (16a).

18a. λx (λy [λz (xRyx & yRyz & zRyx) c] b) a

18b. a has the property being such that b has the property being such that c has the property being such that the first bears R to the second and itself and the second bears R to itself and the third and the third bears R to the second and the first

Thus, one might think, we are driven to the conclusion that the proposition asserted must be cognitively distinct from, but representationally identical to, the enrichment of the semantic content of (16a) *that can be entertained only by one who recognizes the recurrence of a, b, and c.*

But this still isn't convincing. First, there is a natural choice, namely the proposition expressed by (19), which, though structurally different from the semantic content of (17a), is not inordinately complex.[8]

19. λxyz (xRyx & yRyz & zRyx) a,b,c

Second, the proponent of the *recognition of recurrence* analysis of the assertion faces a problem that threatens to make proposition (19) what I asserted, in any case.

The threatened difficulty is best understood by imagining a scenario in which I assertively utter (20), thereby asserting something true and nothing false.

---

[8] Here we are binding triples rather than individual variables.

20. I have only recently believed that aRba & bRbc & cRba.

The imagined context is one in which I recognize all recurrences of the individuals a, b, and c, *despite in the past not recognizing their recurrence when entertaining and believing the bare singular proposition that is the semantic content of the complement clause.* The analysis that incorporates *recognition-of-recurrence* into the proposition asserted explains how it is that I *now* assert something true and nothing false by identifying the proposition my assertion reports me as only recently believing as the proposition that is a *recognition-of-recurrence-requiring* enrichment of the semantic content of the complement clause.

But a problem will arise if we assume that you, my audience, recognize my assertive intention, but do not yourself recognize the recurrence, because you fear you might be in a Peter-'Paderewski' type situation regarding one or more of the names and their bearers. It is not that you are in that situation or that you believe you are; you are just cautious and don't take it for granted that you aren't in it. In this case, you can't discount the possibility that I have wrongly come to take myself to recognize recurrence where there is none. Because of this, you may not be able to entertain the proposition that the recurrence analysis claims I truly asserted, *while remaining confident that it is the proposition I asserted.* For if you don't use the names as I do, and so don't recognize the recurrence, you won't entertain the proposition I in fact did assert (which we here assume to be true). But surely, if I did assert that proposition and you recognized my assertive intention, you ought to be able to answer the question, "What did Scott just assert?," if asked. Moreover, it would seem that you ought be able correctly to do so by uttering (21), with the intention of picking out the precise belief-object I did.

21. Scott said that he has only recently believed that aRba & bRbc & cRba.

What would *you* thereby assert? Presumably not any proposition involving recognition of recurrence, *because you don't recognize recurrence*. Rather, it might seem that the best you might do is to truly assert proposition (22).

22. Scott said: he has only recently believed that λ*xyz (xRyx &*
    yRyz & zRyx) a,b,c

But if *your assertive utterance* of sentence (21) succeeds in asserting proposition (22), then *my original utterance* of (20) must have asserted proposition (23), in which there is no recurrence to recognize.

23. Scott has only recently believed that λ*xyz (xRyx & yRyz &*
    zRyx) a,b,c

Worse, if your assertive utterance *directly* resulted in the assertion of proposition (22), *without the assertion of any RR-requiring proposition involving a, b, and c*, then it could be argued that my assertive utterance *directly* resulted in the assertion of proposition (23) *without the assertion of any RR-requiring proposition involving a, b, and c*. But then the case for *recognition of recurrence* as a Millian mode of presentation in RR-requiring propositions based on seemingly crucial examples like (15) and (20) would be gone.

Because of this, we are not yet able to conclude that there are propositions incorporating *recognition of recurrence* as a Millian mode of presentation that does not change referential content. There is no doubt that recognition of recurrence is crucial to cognition, and to a proper pragmatic account of the propositions asserted or otherwise communicated by uses of language. What remains unresolved at this point is whether such recognition is ever itself a constitutive factor in individuating propositions. Were the problems with the arguments based on (15) and (20) isolated ones, we could

simply leave the question of the existence of RR-requiring propositions open. But the problems aren't isolated; they have counterparts
involving many propositions of limited cognitive accessibility postulated in earlier chapters. These potential problems will be addressed
in the next chapter.

Believing, Asserting, and Communicating Propositions of Limited Accessibility

Ihave argued throughout that if propositions are purely represen-tational cognitive acts, they are capable of incorporating Millian modes of presentation of their constituents. These are ways of iden-tifying predication targets, or properties predicated, when entertain-ing a proposition. Since to entertain p is to perform p, adding such a mode results in a new proposition p* representationally identical to, but cognitively distinct from, p, where to entertain p* is also to en-tertain p, but not conversely. In chapters 2–5, I introduced several ways of cognizing propositional constituents that can be incorpo-rated into propositions without changing referential content; they include (i) entertaining a proposition that is itself a predication tar-get (or a constituent of such a target), (ii) first-person cognition, (iii) present-tense cognition, (iv) linguistic cognition, and (v) perceptual cognition.

Each of these gives rise to propositions cognitive access to which is limited to only some agents otherwise capable of entertaining, af-firming, and believing propositions. With (i), the limitation excludes unsophisticated believers who are unable to make propositions they entertain targets of further predications. With (iv), non–language users are unable to entertain any proposition incorporating a lin-guistic mode of presentation, while language users entertain those that incorporate modes involving expressions with which they are familiar. With (v), the excluded agents are defined by the lack, or temporary nonuse, of particular perceptual modalities. The limitations concerning (ii) and (iii) are of a different order. Every agent x capable of thinking of itself as being one way or another is, I suspect, capable of thinking of itself in a motivationally special (first-person) way that no other agent can use to think of x. Any such agent x, and only x, can entertain a proposition that predicates a property of x, identified in the first-person way. Similarly, every agent capable of thinking of time t, at t, is, I should imagine, capable of thinking of t, at t, in a motivationally special (present-tense) way that no agent can use to think of t at any other time. This means that for each time t, there are propositions that predicate properties of t, identified in the present-tense way, that can be entertained only at t.

In order for propositions incorporating these different Millian modes of presentation to play a role in communication, they must be assertable and, more generally, communicable. This, in turn, requires that it be possible to report these propositions as having been asserted or communicated. As I indicated in chapter 6, this can pose an explanatory problem in communicative situations involving agents with differing cognitive access to the propositions to be communicated. The problem won't typically arise in cases involving (i)—the entertainment of propositions as targets of further predications—because the communication envisioned, involving assertion, reports of assertion, and the like, presupposes that the parties can make the propositions they entertain targets of further predications. The problem also won't usually arise (in a serious way) in cases involving (iv)—the entertainment of propositions involving linguistic modes of presentation—because the paradigm case involves the linguistic communication of speakers using the same language. But the problem does arise for first-person, present-tense, and perceptual Millian modes. Since the problem gave us pause in considering *recognition of recurrence*, a discussion of its implications for these modes of presentation may help resolve our worries.

We can construct a first-person case corresponding to the worrisome case in chapter 6 by considering my use of (1a) to assert something true and nothing false at the denouement of John Perry's messy shopper case, discussed in chapter 3.

1a. Only now do I realize that I made the mess.

The semantic content of this sentence in the context is roughly indicated by (1b).

1b. [Only now has it been so] SS realizes that SS made the mess.

Since (in the imagined scenario) I realized for some time that he (looking at me in the security mirror) made the mess, this proposition is false. What I asserted was not that proposition, but the true, first-person enrichment (1c) resulting from my self-ascription of realizing *in the first-person way* that I made the mess.

1c. [Only just now has it been so] λx [x realizes: λy *(y made the mess)I]* I

Although you, my audience, can't entertain this proposition, you should be able to identify it, while using (2a) to assert something true and nothing false.

2a. *Scott* asserted that only now has *he* realized that *he* made the mess.

What does this involve? First, we take the anaphora to give us (2b).

2b. λx (x asserted [only now has it been so: λy (y realizes: y made the mess) x]) SS

On the assumption that my utterance of (1a) asserted nothing false, (2b), which reports me as having asserted something that is in fact false, is itself false, and so must be pragmatically enriched. The semantic content undergoing enrichment predicates *being true of SS* of a certain propositional function *pf1*. That function assigns to each object o the proposition that predicates *asserting proposition* P_o of o. P_o is the result of applying the operation *only now has it been so* to the proposition P_o^* that predicates *being true of o* to propositional function *pf2*. This propositional function assigns to any object o* the proposition that assigns to each o* the proposition R_{o^*} *that o* realizes that o* made the mess*. R_{o^*} predicates the realizing relation of o* and the proposition $R^*_{o^*}$ that predicates *being one who made the mess* of o*. To get the needed pragmatic enrichment, it is sufficient to substitute $pf2^{1st\text{-}person}$ for *pf2*. Informally put, $pf2^{1st\text{-}person}$ assigns to any o* the proposition $R_{o^*\ 1st\text{-}person}$ *that* o* (identified in the first-person way) *realizes in the first-person way that o* made the mess*. This proposition predicates *realizing* of o* (identified in the first-person way) and the proposition $R^*_{o^*\ 1st\text{-}person}$ that predicates *being one who made the mess* of o*, *identifying o* in the first-person way*.[1]

Although you don't entertain the proposition I asserted, you succeed in identifying and reporting precisely what I asserted. Hence, the communication is, for all intents and purposes, perfect. Two things are crucial to your success. (i) You must have the concept *identifying oneself* in the first-person way. (ii) You must be able to recognize that my assertion reported a cognition of this kind. You are aided in (i) by the fact that you routinely have such cognitions yourself, implicitly recognizing them to be distinct from other cognitions, to be motivationally special, and to involve having a perspective on yourself that no one else has. Not believing yourself to be

---

[1] The parenthesized material doesn't affect the present result and so is optional.

special in this regard, you take it for granted that I also have such cognitions. You are aided in (ii) by the fact that I have used the first-person pronoun, knowing the rule for its use and knowing, in the first-person way, that I am using it. Realizing this, you take me to be reporting a first-person cognition. You identify which cognition it is by combining your grasp of the semantic content of the sentence I used in the context with your knowledge of the conversational background.

The explanation of how *present-tense* cognitions are communicated at different times is essentially the same. Consider again the discussion of the case in chapter 3 in which I plan to attend a meeting I know will start at t—noon, June 13, 2013. Not wanting to be late, I remind myself of this on the morning of June 13th. Still, when I hear the clock strike noon, I utter (3a), and my behavior changes.

3a. The meeting starts now!

Coming to believe of t *in the present-tense way* that the meeting starts then motivates me to hurry off. Had I not believed this, I wouldn't have done so, even though I would have continued to believe, of t, that the meeting starts then. Just as in the first-person case, coming to believe something of my predication target (in this case t) in the special way is coming to believe something new, as indicated by the *truth* of my report (3b) at t.

3b. I only just realized that the meeting starts now!

For this report to be true, the proposition $P_{t\ present\text{-}tense}$ to which I only just came to bear the *realizing* relation must be one that predicates *starting at t* of the meeting, the entertainment of which requires t to be cognized *in the present-tense way*. As in the first-person case, the semantic content of the sentence I uttered is false. That content is the singular proposition (3c).

3c. [Only just now has it been so that] SS realizes that the meet-
     ing starts at t

Substituting $P_{t \text{ present-tense}}$ for the bare singular proposition P_t that the
meeting starts at t gives me a true proposition, represented by (3d),
which I assert.[2]

3d. [Only just now has it been so that] SS realizes: the meeting
     starts at t (identified in the present-tense way)

In this case there is no problem in you, my audience, entertaining
the same proposition at t that I entertain and assert at t. If you wish
to report my assertion, you can do so by uttering (3e)—using 'starts
now' at t or 'started then' later.

3e. *SS* asserted that *he* only just realized that the meeting starts
     now/started then.
     λx (x asserted that x only just realized that the meeting starts
     at t) SS

The proposition asserted by your utterance predicates *being true of
SS* of the propositional function *pf* that assigns to an object o the
proposition that, at t but not before t, o realized *that the meeting
started at t, identifying t in the present-tense way*. In so doing, you identify and report precisely what I asserted, whether or not you can
entertain that proposition at the time of your report. You can do so
because (i) you have the concept *identifying a time t at t* in the special
present-tense way that is available at any time t', and only at t', to
pick out t', and (ii) you recognize that my assertion reported a

---

[2] Of course, since my utterance was first-person, I also asserted the first-person
enrichment of (3d)—*[Only just now has it been so that]* λx (x realize: the meeting starts
at t (identified in the present tense way)) SS (identified in the first-person way)). But this
doesn't change the issues discussed here in any way, and so can be ignored in what
follows.

cognition of this sort. You are aided in (ii) by the fact that I used 'now' and a present-tense construction, presumably knowing their rules of use, and knowing, in the present-tense way, that I was using them. Realizing this, you took me to be reporting a present-tense cognition, which you identified.

The next Millian mode is perception. Recall the example from chapter 5 in which agent A watches a bird, B, hop from branch to branch. A predicates first one, then another other property of B, identified visually. To perform these acts, and so to entertain the propositions, requires identifying one's predication target visually. In specifying the case, I stipulated that B was Tom's pet cardinal, which he had previously told A about—perhaps by uttering 'B is my pet cardinal'. Nevertheless, A is surprised while observing B for the first time when you point at B and say, "That is Tom's pet cardinal." To this A responds by uttering (4a).

4a. I didn't realize that it [demonstrating B] was Tom's pet.

The intuitively plausible result to be preserved is that in so doing A asserts something true and nothing false. Since the false proposition (4b) is semantically expressed by (4a), neither it nor its first-person variant (4c) is asserted.

4b. $\sim$ prior to t (i.e., the time A referred to), A realized B was Tom's pet.

4c. λx [$\sim$ prior to t, x realized B was Tom's pet] A (identified in the first-person way)

Rather, the truths asserted are (4b +) and (4c +).

4b + . $\sim$ prior to t, A realized B (identified visually) was Tom's pet

4c + . λx [$\sim$ prior to t, x realized B (identified visually) was Tom's pet] A (identified in the first-person way)

Since the first-person aspect of A's assertion is not at issue here, I will concentrate only on (4b+), which you, A's audience, can also entertain, affirm, or deny. This facilitates your communication with A, and with others who may be perceiving B.

Suppose, however, you wish to report A's assertion (made when watching B) to someone not perceiving B, or even to recall it yourself later when you aren't perceiving B. You ought to be able to do so using (5a), the semantic content of which is represented by (5b).

5a. While watching B at t, A said that he hadn't realized that B was Tom's pet.

5b. (While watching B at t) λx [x said: $\sim$ prior to t, x realized: B was Tom's pet] A

Since proposition (5b) is false (on the supposition that A's utterance at t asserted something true and nothing false), the proposition you assert in reporting A's attitude must be an enrichment of (5b). Whereas (5b) predicates *being true of A* of a propositional function *pf1* that assigns to o the proposition that o asserted that o hadn't, prior to t, borne the realizing relation to the bare singular proposition that predicates *being Tom's pet* of B, the proposition asserted by your use of (5a) predicates *being true of A* to a related propositional function *pf2* that differs from *pf1* in requiring B to be identified perceptually. That attitude ascription is true.

As before, this explanation depends on two assumptions: (i) that you have the concept *identifying a predication target perceptually* and (ii) that you recognize A's use of (4a) as reporting a cognition of this kind. There is no question that, within limits, most language users satisfy assumptions corresponding to (i) and (ii). We do know what it is to perceive something, realizing that what we can affirm about an object is often affected by whether we are perceiving it. It is no surprise that we can know of an object that it is F by being told, even though we can't always, when perceiving that object, determine that it is F. This is what drives our reaction to the example. For this truism to affect our assessment of what A asserted, and what others report A as asserting, perception must be recognized as a Millian mode of presentation.

Although our communication of truths about propositions we don't entertain is an important aspect of our linguistic practice, our ability to so communicate is limited. If we lack a sensory modality S, we can characterize others as bearing attitudes to propositions incorporating S only if we understand S and the role it plays in their cognition well enough to identify those propositions. Even when we share a sensory modality such as vision, some fine-grained ways of visually cognizing predication targets in propositional attitudes may resist identification by outsiders (or explicit verbal encoding by the agent)—making it practically impossible to communicate the propositions in question. These limitations on our ability to understand ourselves and others are inherent in the cognitions involved in an important class of propositional attitudes. They do not, however, obscure the abilities we do have, and the ways in which we use language to express, identify, and report agents' attitudes to propositions of limited accessibility.

We can now resolve the difficulty left hanging at the end of chapter 6. The question is whether *recognition of recurrence* is a Millian mode of presentation distinguishing propositions that incorporate it from their representationally identical counterparts. The difficulty posed for resolving this question arose in a context in which I assertively utter (6), thereby asserting something true and nothing false.

6.   I have only recently believed that aRba & bRbc & cRba.

The context is one in which I recognize all recurrences of individuals a, b, and c, despite not recognizing their recurrence in the past when entertaining and believing the bare singular proposition p semantically expressed by the complement clause. An analysis incorporating *recognition-of-recurrence* in the proposition asserted explains the truth of my report by identifying the proposition I report myself as only recently believing as an enrichment of p that requires *recognition of the recurrence of a, b, and c*. The threat to this analysis arose from assuming that you, my audience, recognize my assertive intention, without yourself recognizing the recurrence because you fear you might be in a Peter-'Paderewski'–type situation regarding one or more of the names and their bearers. As I previously indicated, you need not believe you are in that situation; it is enough if you are simply cautious and don't take it for granted that you aren't. This prevents you from entertaining the RR-proposition of limited accessibility that the analysis claims I asserted while at the same time feeling confident that your report captures my intention. But surely, if I did assert it and you recognized my intention, you ought to be able to correctly answer the question, "What did Scott just assert?," using (7a), with the right intention.

7a. *Scott* said that *he* has only recently believed that aRba & bRbc & cRba.

What proposition would you thereby truly assert, given that it is not one the entertainment of which requires you to recognize the recurrence of a, b, c? As the discussion of the earlier examples in this chapter makes clear, it should be a certain pragmatic enrichment of the semantic content (7b) of (7a).

7b. λx (x said: [only recently has it been so: x believes aRba & bRbc & cRba]) SS

The semantic content undergoing enrichment predicates *being true of SS* of a propositional function *pf* that assigns to each object o the proposition that predicates *asserting proposition* P_o of o. P_o is the result of applying the operation *only recently has it been so* to the proposition P_o* *that* o *believes that aRba & bRbc & cRba*. P_o* predicates *believing* of o and the proposition P^C that is the conjunction of the proposition predicating R of the triple a,b,a, the proposition predicating R of the triple b,b,c, and the proposition predicating R of the triple c,b,a. The needed pragmatic enrichment substitutes a new propositional function *pf*^{RR} for *pf*. The function *pf*^{RR} assigns to any object o the proposition P^{RR}_o* *that* o *believes that aRba & bRbc & cRba (recognizing the recurrence of a,b,c)*. This proposition predicates *believing* of o and the proposition P^{CRR} that enriches the conjunction P^C by requiring one who entertains it to recognize the recurrence of a, b, and c.

In this way, you succeed in identifying and reporting precisely what I asserted, without yourself entertaining the proposition I asserted. As in other cases of this sort, the communication is successful. Also as in other cases, two things are crucial for you to be able to perform the needed enrichment: (i) you must have the concept of a cognition in which one *recognizes the recurrence of elements*; (ii) something about my utterance must tip you to the fact that the cognition I am reporting is a cognition of that type.

Regarding (i), *recognition of recurrence* is, without doubt, an important form of cognition for most cognitive agents. Of course, not all agents who recognize recurrence have the concept *recognizing recurrence*. Having it, I suspect, requires some sophistication. Still, it is plausible that ordinary-language users do have the concept and explicitly employ it on some occasions, for example when judging whether others do or do not recognize the same word recurring in a text or dialogue. Since recognizing recurrences of words one understands in sentences is closely related to recognizing recurrences of the contributions the words make to what the sentences are used to express, condition (i) seems to be satisfied.

As for condition (ii), although recurrence of a word—e.g., a name or a predicate—used by a speaker is not always recognized by those who understand the word, it usually is. Because it is, a hearer who understands the word and recognizes its recurrence in a speaker's remarks is often justified in taking the speaker to recognize the recurrence of content. As I argued in chapter 6, this is not always enough to justify taking the proposition asserted by a speaker to encode such recognition.[3] But the context of utterance and the nature of the sentence uttered will often provide the extra information needed to resolve uncertainty about whether the proposition asserted incorporates recognition or recurrence. Thus, I am inclined to think that condition (ii) is also satisfied.

This dissolves the objection at the end of chapter 6 to taking *recognition of recurrence* to be a genuine Millian mode of presentation that distinguishes propositions incorporating it from representationally identical propositions that do not. Having reached this point, we interpret my assertive utterance of

6. I have only recently believed that aRba & bRbc & cRba.

as asserting a proposition that predicates only recently believing of me and the proposition *that aRba & bRbc & cRba (the entertainment of which requires recognition of the recurrences of a, b, and c).* We further interpret your assertive utterance of

7a. *Scott* said that *he* has only recently believed that aRba & bRbc & cRba.

as reporting me as having asserted precisely that proposition, even if you do not recognize the recurrence yourself, and so are not in a position to entertain the proposition you report me as believing.

---

[3] See examples 5–9 of chapter 6.

Since (8) is a trivial, cognitively accessible consequence of what I asserted in uttering (6), I also count as having asserted it.

8. SS has only recently believed that λxyz *(xRyx & yRyz & zRyx)* a,b,c.

For a similar reason, it is plausible to take your utterance of (7a) to count as also asserting (9).

9. SS said: he has only recently believed that λxyz *(xRyx & yRyz & zRyx)* a,b,c.

However, these results are no threat to the *recognition-of-recurrence* analysis of what I asserted, and what you asserted in reporting my assertion. Rather, (8) and (9) are now seen, not as alternatives to the analysis, but as consequences of it.

CHAPTER 8

Recognition of Recurrence Revisited

In the last two chapters, I have argued, first, that there is a pragmatic notion of *recognition* of the recurrence of a propositional constituent throughout different presentations of it, and second, that because propositions are purely representational cognitive acts, we can distinguish representationally identical propositions that differ as to whether performing those acts (entertaining those propositions) requires one to recognize recurrences of propositional constituents, requires one not to recognize recurrences, or imposes no requirement of recognition or nonrecognition of recurrences. We have seen that which of these propositions one accepts can markedly affect the rationally justified inferences one is able to draw. We have also seen that, in addition to justifying inferences by cognitively unifying different occurrences of the same content within a proposition, recognition justifies inferences that require the agent to recognize recurrences of the same contents across different premises, and across premises and conclusions. Finally, I have argued that although *recognition of recurrence* can play a role in resolving some instances of Frege's puzzle, it is not an all-purpose solution, but merely one useful instrument in our pragmatic tool kit.[1] In this chapter I will use *recognition of recurrence* to shed light on two related puzzles about quantification.

[1] For further discussion see Soames (2012).

A PUZZLE INVOLVING QUANTIFICATION AND RECURRENCE IN SINGULAR THOUGHT

The first puzzle, presented in Alonzo Church (1988), uses the seemingly plausible premise that *for any object x, no one believes that x isn't x* plus a widely accepted axiom schema of quantification theory to derive the incredible conclusion that *for any objects x and y, if anyone believes that x isn't y, then x really isn't y*. Here is the derivation.

(i)   For all x, y (x = y $\supset$ (Fx $\supset$ Fy) (Axiom Schema of Quantification Theory)

(ii) $\forall$x,y (x = y $\supset$ ($\sim$ Jones believes that x $\neq$ x $\supset$ $\sim$ Jones believes that x $\neq$ y))

(iii) $\forall$x,y ($\sim$ Jones believes that x $\neq$ x $\supset$ (x = y $\supset$ $\sim$ Jones believe that x $\neq$ y))

(iv) $\forall$x $\sim$ (Jones believes that x $\neq$ x)

(v) $\forall$x,y (Jones believes that x $\neq$ y $\supset$ x $\neq$ y)

Clearly, something has gone wrong. Suppose Jones has amnesia and believes that he's not Jones. Since he is Jones, this seems to falsify (v). Similarly, suppose that the actor Ed Norton, whom Jones has heard of, introduces himself to Jones as "Ed Norton." Thinking he is an imposter, Jones tells his neighbor, "He isn't Ed Norton." It would seem that Jones thereby believes that *he (Ed Norton) isn't Ed Norton*. But surely, it doesn't follow that *he isn't Ed Norton*.

The culprit is (iv). When Jones has amnesia, Jones predicates *nonidentity* of himself, identified in the first-person way, and Jones, identified another way, *not recognizing his recurrence*. Since Jones endorses the predication, Jones believes the proposition. Jones also counts as believing the distinct but representationally identical proposition in which nonidentity is predicated of Jones and Jones, no matter how Jones is identified as first and second argument of the relation. Since Jones believes that he is not Jones, there is someone x (Jones) such that Jones believes that x isn't x. Similar remarks apply to the Norton example.

Why, then, did (iv) seem plausible? One who encounters 'Jones is Jones', who understands it, and who recognizes the recurrence of the name will accept it. Such an agent thereby endorses both a bare singular proposition predicating identity of Jones and Jones and a representationally identical proposition requiring recognition of recurrence. The agent will also reject negations of these propositions. But, whereas the recognition-free negative identity claim can be presented in another way in which it is accepted and believed, its recognition-requiring counterpart can't be. *No one believes it.* On this (enriched recognition-requiring) understanding, it is true both that *no one believes that Jones isn't* Jones and that *someone x* (namely Jones) *is such that no one believes x not to be x.*

So there is a plausible way of understanding (iv) on which it is true. But if we impose this understanding of (iv) on other steps in the argument, then either schema (i) will fail—which will happen if we *don't* also impose a recognition requirement on recurrences of an object designated by 'x' and 'y' relative to assignments that treat them the same—or conclusion (v) will become uninteresting—which will happen if we *do* uniformly impose such a requirement even when the variables are different. Either way, the puzzle is disarmed.

MORE ON QUANTIFICATION AND RECOGNITION OF RECURRENCE

One of the examples I used in chapter 6 to argue that recognition of recurrence is not semantically encoded was (1a).

1a. John fooled Mary into believing that he, John, wasn't John.

Typically, one who uses (1a) will recognize John recurring in the proposition asserted. But since it would be absurd to ascribe to Mary belief in a proposition from which it could trivially be inferred *that John is non-self-identical*, the proposition she is reported to believe is the negation of one that predicates identity of John and John, *without requiring recognition of recurrence*. If the semantic content of the clause required such recognition, the proposition semantically encoded by (1a) would be transparently absurd, which it isn't.

Since what (1a) tells us to be true of John must be true of someone, (1b) should also be true, which it will be if the proposition expressed by the complement of 'believe' relative to an assignment of a value to the variable doesn't require recognition of recurrence.

1b. Some man Mary met fooled her into believing that he, that man, wasn't that man.

Some x: Mary met x [x fooled Mary into believing that x isn't x]

Though this is correct, it's not the whole story. There are, I believe, contexts in which an assertive utterance (2a) would express something true (and nothing false), even though an utterance of (2b) would express something false, and a corresponding utterance of (2c) would express a truth.

2a. Because Mary only recently came to believe *that Venus was a planet in the solar system and Venus was smaller than Earth*, she only recently came to believe that some planet in the solar system was smaller than Earth.[2]

2b. Because Mary only recently came to believe that *Hesperus was a planet in the solar system and Phosphorus was smaller than*

---

[2] Assume, for the sake of argument, that Mary is ignorant about Mars and Mercury.

Earth, she only recently came to believe that some planet in the solar system was smaller than Earth.

2c. It is not the case that because Mary only recently came to believe *that Hesperus was a planet in the solar system and Phosphorus was smaller than Earth*, she only recently came to believe that some planet in the solar system was smaller than Earth.

The truth of the use of (2a) might be explained by taking the agent's use of the italicized clause to contribute a proposition p_R, requiring recognition of the recurrence of Venus, to the assertion made by the utterance. The falsity of a corresponding use of (2b), as well as the truth of (2c), could then be explained by taking the contribution of the corresponding clause in these cases to be representationally identical to, but cognitively distinct from, p_R. The most natural choice is a proposition requiring nonrecognition of the recurrence of Venus, but the explanation could go through even if the proposition contributed were neutral as to recognition or nonrecognition.

Now notice the relationship between (2a) and (2d).[3]

2d. For some x, because Mary only recently came to believe *that x was a planet in the solar system and x was smaller than Earth*, she only recently came to believe that some planet in the solar system was smaller than Earth.

Since we may use (2d) to say about something what we use (2a) to truly say about Venus, it should be possible, and even natural, to use (2d) to assert a truth (in the same context we imagined for (2a)). To account for this we may allow pragmatic enrichment in

---

[3] Read 'some planet' in (2d) as taking small scope relative to 'believe'.

quantified cases as we do in non-quantified cases.[4] The *semantic content* of (2d) is defined (in part) in terms of a propositional function *pf* that assigns to arbitrary o the proposition that predicates *belief* of Mary and the conjunction of the proposition that o is a planet and o is smaller than Earth. Since this conjunctive proposition *doesn't* require recognition of recurrence of o, the proposition *semantically expressed* by (2d) is liable to be false. By contrast, the *enriched proposition* we may use (2d) to assert substitutes a propositional function pf^{RR} that differs from *pf* only in requiring recognition of recurrence of o in the conjunctive proposition. This asserted proposition is true.

At this point it is worth observing that (2e) bears a relation to (2c) that is similar to the relation (2d) bears to (2a).

2e. For some x,y such that x = y, it is not the case that because Mary only recently came to believe *that x was a planet in the solar system and y was smaller than Earth,* she only recently came to believe that some planet in the solar system was smaller than Earth.

So, it would seem that what we could use (2c) to truly say about Hesperus and Phosphorus we could use (2e) to truly say about some pair of identical things. Here, the semantic content of the italicized clause is the propositional function pf_2 that maps pairs of objects o_1, o_2 onto the proposition that o_1 is a planet in the solar system and o_2 is smaller than Earth. It is *not* enriched by a requirement requiring recognition of recurrence when $o_1 = o_2$—though, depending on how we treated (2b,c), we may enrich requiring *nonrecognition* in that case.

---

[4] As we did in the previous section when discussing ways in which the steps in Church's argument can be taken.

This analysis gives us a way of making the propositions that (2d) and (2e) are used to assert jointly true in the sort of contexts imagined. This, in turn, shows that schematic statements of Leibniz's Law along the lines of (3a) can fail in a certain sense.

3a. $\forall x \forall y \ (x = y \supset (Fx \leftrightarrow Fy))$ [where Fx differs from Fy by containing one or more free occurrences of 'x' where Fy contains occurrences of 'x']

To adopt a schema is to be committed to the truth of its instances. If the truth of an instance is the truth of the proposition it semantically expresses, nothing I have said conflicts with adopting (3a). But one must be careful not to identify the *semantic content of an instance* with the proposition it would be used to assert on various occasions. Some of these propositions may be false. Though perhaps surprising, there is nothing to fear from this result, which is perfectly consistent with the statement of Leibniz's Law given by (3b).[5]

3b. For all x, y, if x is identical with y, then any property of x is a property of y.

DEALING WITH A RESIDUAL WORRY

Finally, I address a version of a worry I have raised elsewhere in another form.[6] Recognizing recurrences of an object through different presentations makes sense only if the presentations really do present the same thing. One can't *recognize* an occurrence of y as a recurrence of x, unless y is x. One can, of course, *take x to be y*, when x *isn't* y. Some such cases may even be indistinguishable to the agent from genuine cases of recognition. Given this, one must, it would

---

[5] The explanation of how (3b) can be true even if some instances of (3a) are false is explained on pp. 439–40 of Soames (2014c).

[6] See the penultimate section of chapter 6 of King, Soames, and Speaks (2014).

seem, acknowledge purely representational cognitive acts in which one predicates a relation R of distinct things x and y, *wrongly treating x as recurring.*

Are these representational acts genuine propositions? Suppose that when cognizing Cicero's twin brother C + one mistakenly takes oneself to have recognized Cicero. Suppose further that one does this in the service of predicating *that x shaves y* of the pair of Cicero and C +, taking oneself to "recognize" recurrence. Finally, suppose that, in fact, each brother shaves the other but neither shaves himself. Is this cognitive act a proposition? If so, is it true? If it is a proposition, and if, as I have supposed, the truth conditions of a proposition are read off what it predicates of what, then it must be true. But is it a proposition? The problem is that it *requires* one who performs it to *mistake* one thing for another. Since I doubt that restrictions encoded by genuine propositions concerning how their predication targets are identified can require *inherent misapprehensions*, I doubt that such acts are propositions. I doubt this because I take special sub-acts that are particular ways of identifying predication targets to be constituents of genuine propositions only when they are the means by which one *successfully* identifies those targets. Since misidentification doesn't contribute to such success, it is not, I think, a genuine Millian mode of presentation by which propositions can be individuated. The alternative would be to regard such acts as degenerate propositions, while recognizing that they play no important role in our theories of language and mind. Though there are propositions like that, I now suspect that cognitive acts involving misapprehensions of recurrence are not among them.

Situating Cognitive Propositions
in a Broader Context

In chapters 2–8, I noted several restrictions propositions can impose on how their predication targets must be cognized by those who entertain them. For each restriction there are pairs of distinct but representationally identical propositions with the same structure and constituents, differing only in that one imposes the restriction but the other doesn't. One who entertains, endorses, or believes a proposition consisting of the predication of a property of a target that must be identified in a restricted way, thereby also entertains, endorses, or believes the corresponding proposition without the restriction. In chapters 6–8, I related my conception of representationally identical but cognitively distinct propositions to the distinction in Fine (2007) between *coordinated* and *uncoordinated* propositions, which are cognitively distinct but representationally identical, while relating my treatment of *recognition of recurrence* as a Millian mode of presentation to its treatment in Fine (2007) and Salmon (2012). In this chapter, I will relate other Millian modes of presentation to earlier work on Frege's puzzle, broadly conceived, by David Kaplan, John Perry, Nathan Salmon, David Lewis, Hilary Putnam, Saul Kripke, and others.

FREGE'S PUZZLE: NONDESCRIPTIONALITY, DIRECT REFERENCE, AND THE ESSENTIAL INDEXICAL

Prior to the seminal work of Kripke, Putnam, and others on names and natural kind terms, the conventional wisdom about sense and reference embraced theses T1 and T2.[1]

T1. The sense, or meaning, of a term both differs from and determines its referent (at a world-state).

T2. Because codesignative terms often differ in meaning, substitution of one for another often changes the meaning of a sentence, the assertion it is used to make, and the beliefs it is used to express.

After Kripke and Putnam it appeared that no plausible assignment of *descriptive meanings* to names and natural kind terms could vindicate T1 and T2. Although this led both to give up T1, neither gave up T2, despite being unable to provide a plausible nondescriptive conception of meaning that would vindicate it. Initially, Kripke wrote as if it were clear that some version of T2 was true, while remaining silent about what, other than their designata, names and natural kind terms contribute to the meanings of sentences containing them, or to the assertions made and beliefs expressed using them.[2] This was perplexing. Could a satisfying account of meaning be found that validates T2, or should T2 also be given up?

David Kaplan was among the first to advance the discussion, by implicitly casting doubt on T2. Writing in Kaplan (1979, 1989) on

---

[1] Kripke (1972), Putnam (1970, 1973, 1975). See also Burgess (1996).
[2] See Soames (2011) for discussion.

"pure indexicals"—'I', 'now', 'here', 'actually', etc.—and demonstratives—'he', 'she', 'that', ⌈that F⌉, etc.—he distinguished between the *character*, or linguistic meaning, of an expression and its *semantic content* relative to a context of utterance.[3] For Kaplan, a context C consists of a *circumstance of evaluation* EV_C (which is a pair of a time and a world-state) plus a designated agent and location. For most (but not all) of his purposes, the agent can be taken to be *the user of an expression* and the location can be identified with the user's location. The character of an expression E is a function from contexts C to semantic contents of E at C, which are functions from circumstances EV to extensions (designations) of E at those circumstances. When E is a simple indexical (including any of those listed above), this second function assigns the extension of E at EV_C as its extension in all circumstances. So simple indexicals are rigid designators (their referents don't change from circumstance to circumstance once the context is fixed). Moreover, the *semantic content* of a simple indexical E_1 at context C_1 is identical with the semantic content of a simple indexical E_2 at context C_2 iff the referent (extension) of E_1 at C_1 is the same as the referent (extension) of E_2 at C_2 (from which it follows that the indexicals with the same referent at C have the same semantic content at C).

If this sounds a bit convoluted, it is—partly because of an inherent tension between Kaplan's goals of simultaneously giving us both a formal logic and a semantics of indexicals and partly because he presented his semantic theory in the then orthodox form of a *theory of truth* relative to a set of parameters.[4] Putting these complications

---

[3] Both Kaplan (1979) and Kaplan (1989) circulated widely long before publication (from the early to mid-1970s onward). Unlike pure indexicals, occurrences of demonstratives were thought to require supplementation by demonstrations. For further discussion of this point, including difficulties and challenges raised by it, see Salmon (2002), and Soames (2010a), pp. 102–5, 147–51, 164–65.

[4] See Soames (2010a), pp. 93–105.

aside, we can take the Kaplanian semantic content of a simple term E at C to be its referent at C, which it contributes to the structured proposition expressed at C by sentences containing E (which may then be evaluated at arbitrary counterfactual circumstances).[5] We call E *directly referential* iff for all contexts C, its semantic content at C is its referent at C. For Kaplan, all proper names and all simple indexicals are directly referential. Since names aren't context sensitive, their semantic contents are fixed across contexts, and so can be identified with their meanings. Thus, whereas Kripke was agnostic about whether coreferential names have the same meanings, Kaplan wasn't; for him, they did.

The significance of these views for Frege's puzzle is mixed.[6] First consider (1) and (2).

1a. I am Scott Soames. (said by SS)
1b. Scott Soames is Scott Soames.
2a. My pants are on fire. (said by SS)
2b. His pants are on fire. (said by someone demonstrating SS)

In both cases, the proposition semantically expressed by (a) at the relevant context C is the proposition semantically expressed by (b), at C. Nevertheless, one who understands (knows the meanings of) both sentences might easily find an utterance of (a) informative in a way that an utterance of (b) isn't. In the case of (1a), those addressed will take themselves to be informed that the one addressing them is SS, while those addressed by someone who utters (1b) will not. The situation with (2) is similar. Although I would feel immediate cause

---

[5] Semantics of this sort are presented in Salmon (1986) and Soames (1987).

[6] To the extent that Kaplan had views at the time about the implication of Frege's puzzle for names, they took the form of an early version of the semantic relationism of Fine (2007). Kaplan articulated his take on the matter in an unpublished lecture in the late 1980s entitled "Word and Belief."

for concern if I were to sincerely accept (2a), I might not be concerned if, looking at myself reflected at an unusual angle in store window, I came to accept my own use of (2b), or if I were to accept someone else's use of (2b) (demonstrating an individual who, in fact, was me). The lesson for Frege's puzzle was that when indexicals are involved (and hence when linguistic meaning diverges from semantic content), differences in informativeness (of the sort illustrated here) are compatible with sameness of semantic content.

Welcome as it was, this result didn't go nearly far enough. For one thing, it didn't address instances of Frege's puzzle involving proper names or natural kind terms rather than indexicals.[7] For another, it didn't tell us what assertions are made by uses of the (a) and (b) sentences in (1) and (2), or what beliefs they are used to express. Nor did it address instances of Frege's puzzle involving propositional attitude ascriptions, as illustrated by (3) and (4).

3a. They believed/asserted that I was Scott Soames. (said by SS)
3b. They believed/asserted that Scott Soames was Scott Soames.
4a. I believed/asserted that my pants were on fire. (said by SS)
4b. I believed/asserted that his pants were on fire. (said by me, demonstrating SS)

It seems obvious that uses of the (a) and (b) sentences in (1) and (2) can assert different things, and that uses the (a) and (b) sentences in (3) and (4) can differ in truth value, despite the fact that the Kaplanian propositions semantically expressed at the contexts in question are the same. Thus, Frege's puzzle remained in force.

---

[7] The approach that came to be known as *semantic two-dimensionalism* attempted to deal with this problem by analyzing names and natural kind terms as indexically rigidified descriptions, associating sentences containing them with pairs of propositions, and adopting complicated analyses of attitude verbs as operating on these pairs. For leading ideas, see Chalmers (1996, 2002, 2011) and Jackson (1998a, 1998b, 2007). For criticism, see Soames (2005c, 2006a, 2007b).

At this point two important articles, Perry (1977, 1979), appeared. In addition to reinforcing T3 and T4, two main tenets of Kaplan's theory of indexicals, these articles emphasized the problems indexicals pose for Fregean conceptions of language, including the glaring difficulties posed by beliefs expressed and assertions made using the first-person singular pronoun.

> T3. Referents of uses of indexicals are not descriptively fixed by purely qualitative contents in the minds of their users.
>
> T4. Uses of indexicals do not contribute their meanings to propositions expressed by uses of sentences containing them; what they do contribute to those propositions are the referents of the indexicals in the contexts of use.

The following passage, building on T3 and T4, illustrates the problem of first-person belief.

> Let us imagine David Hume, alone in his study, on a particular afternoon in 1775, thinking to himself, "I wrote the *Treatise*." Can anyone *else* apprehend the thought he apprehended by thinking this? First note that what he thinks is true. So no one could apprehend the same thought, unless they apprehended a true thought. Now suppose Heimson is a bit crazy, and thinks himself to be David Hume. Alone in his study, he says to himself, "I wrote the *Treatise*." However much his inner life may, at that moment, resemble Hume's on that afternoon in 1775, the fact remains: Hume was right and Heimson was wrong. Heimson cannot think the very thought that Hume thought to himself, by using that very sentence.[8]

---

[8] Perry (1977), p. 487.

This description of the case is clearly correct. Moreover, as Perry effectively argued, if we restrict ourselves to purely qualitative, descriptive thoughts (propositions)—e.g., *that the so-and-so wrote the Treatise*—we can find no thought that is both one Heimson can entertain and what Hume expressed using "I wrote the *Treatise*." This left two alternatives. Either the thought (proposition) Hume expressed can't be entertained by Heimson or anyone else, or it is a thought others can entertain, but not by using "I wrote the *Treatise*."

Rightly attributing the first alternative to Frege, Perry gave arguments A1 and A2 against it.

A1. Although each of us is acquainted with himself or herself in a way no one else is, we do not pick ourselves out via qualitative Fregean senses that are unavailable to others, yet known by us to apply uniquely to ourselves.

A2. Although beliefs about the present time expressed using 'now' or the present tense pose the same sort of problem that first-person beliefs do, they can't be treated by positing "for each time, a primitive and particular way in which it is presented to us at that time, which gives rise to thoughts accessible only at that time, and expressible, at that time, with 'now'."[9]

Later in this chapter I will discuss Saul Kripke's challenge to A1 (and by extension to A2) based on an enlightening expansion of Frege's notion of sense to include *acquaintance-based senses*. Since I don't, in the end, think this reconstruction of Frege will do, I agree with Perry that Fregean conceptions of propositions of limited accessibility

---

[9] Ibid., p. 491. In this quote Perry uses the word 'thoughts' to designate what is thought or believed, i.e., propositions. This bears watching, since he doesn't always do so, but rather sometimes uses it to speak of cognitive states, acts, or events of believing.

should be rejected. However, this critique does *not* extend to the cognitive conception of propositions, which, by allowing representationally identical but cognitively distinct propositions with the same structure and constituents, avoids the objectionable features of inaccessible Fregean thoughts.

Without the cognitive conception, Perry concluded that what makes first-person and present-tense beliefs distinctive are *not* the propositions believed, but the special first-person, present-tense *ways of believing* propositions that can also be believed in other ways. On this view, anyone can at any time believe the proposition that I am working now—i.e., the proposition that SS is working at 2 PM, January 1, 2014 (PST)—but only I (SS) can do so by thinking "I am working now," and I can do it only on January 1, 2014. All right, but what are propositions and what are ways of believing them?

In Perry (1977, 1979) propositions are essentially Russellian combinations of propositions and objects. This conception make no room for representationally identical but cognitively distinct propositions with the same structure and constituents—e.g., the cognitive proposition I express by uttering "I am working now" at t and the proposition that SS is working at t.[10] For Perry, ways of believing Russellian propositions were, to a first approximation, types of cognitive states, acts, or events in the mental lives of agents who understand and accept sentence meanings, conceived of as Kaplanian characters.[11] On this view, for me to believe, at the present time t, the proposition p—*that I am working now*—is *not* for me to believe a proposition of limited accessibility, but simply for me to believe p— *that SS is working at t*—by virtue of accepting a sentence (or mental

---

[10] See Perry (1977), pp. 494, 496.

[11] Although Perry's term for such meanings is 'role', he grants in Perry (1977), p. 493, fn. 6, that his notion *role* is similar to Kaplan's *character*. See also pp. 479–81, 493–95.

representation) at t with the same meaning or character M as the English sentence "I am working now." Although p is fully accessible to other agents A*, and at other times t*, it cannot be believed by A*, or at t*, by accepting M. To believe p, A* must accept some distinct M* that expresses p at contexts with A* as agent and t* as time.

There are three main problems with this positive account.

Problem 1: The characterization of first-person, present-tense belief is too linguistic. Since such belief is not the special province of language users, some nonlinguistic characterization is needed.

Problem 2: Being true to our pretheoretic ascriptions of first-person beliefs to others, and of present-tense beliefs involving other times, while also being true to our use of such ascriptions in explaining actions, requires a conception of propositions according to which to believe old propositions in first-person and present-tense ways *is* thereby to believe new propositions too. Because Perry lacked such a conception, he claimed that *"We use senses [Kaplanian characters] to individuate psychological states, in explaining and predicting action. It is the sense entertained [i.e., the Kaplanian character accepted] and not the thought [proposition] apprehended, that is tied to human action."*[12] This is, at best, a highly revisionary error theory that labels much of our pretheoretic thought and talk about belief and action as false, and so in need of systematic correction. Such results shouldn't be accepted unless we are driven to them.

---

[12] Perry (1977), p. 494. The last four pages of Perry (1979) expand on the idea of explaining action in terms of *belief states* individuated by Kaplan-style characters, which in turn are distinguished from the propositions believed by virtue of being in those states.

Problem 3: Problem 2 generalizes to propositional attitudes of all
types; it is not just belief ascriptions but attitude ascriptions of all types that require systematic correction, if
Perry's positive account is accepted. Problem 2 also
generalizes to other—e.g., perceptual and linguistic—
modes of presentation that have nothing to do with Kaplanian characters, or with sentence meanings.

The error theory mentioned in Problem 2 is made more graphic
in Perry (1979). There Perry develops an arresting set of examples
using indexicals—'I', 'now', 'this', and 'that'—in which accurate descriptions and explanations of the actions, inquiries, beliefs, and dis-
agreements of agents require the use of indexicals in the content
clauses of attitude verbs. In these cases, the use of indexicals seems
to be "essential" to specify what is believed, questioned, known, or
unknown. So effective is Perry in constructing the cases that some
readers missed his main point—namely, that despite appearances, it
is an *illusion* to think that indexicals are essential in this way. Perry's
indexicals *are* essential to his *attitude reports*, but, he argues, they are
not essential in specifying *what is believed, questioned, known*, etc.

Perry rightly maintains that his indexicals could be essential to
specifying the propositions to which his agents bear the reported
attitudes only if the latter were propositions of limited accessibility,
which ordinary Russellian and Fregean propositions aren't. Although
Perry admits that he has no conclusive argument against propositions that are somehow inaccessible in principle, he rejects them
because he has no clear idea of what they could possibly be. He says:

[The acceptability or attractiveness of a theory of propositions
of limited accessibility] will depend on other parts of one's
metaphysics; if one finds plausible reasons elsewhere for believing in a universe that has, in addition to our common

world, myriads of private perspectives, the idea of propositions of limited accessibility will fit right in. I have no knock-
down argument against such propositions, or the metaphysical
schemes that find room for them. But I believe only in a common actual world.[13]

This was, I think, a natural and understandable failure of imagi-
nation. If it were true that propositions of limited accessibility required metaphysics going beyond "our common world," they would,
I suppose, be suspect. But, as I have argued, they don't. All of us,
Perry included, believe we have direct private ways of being aware
of ourselves—and of what we are thinking, feeling, or experiencing—
that *others* can't use to become aware of *us,* or those aspects of us.
Since it's not impossible for them to be aware, in a different way, of
what we are directly aware of, recognizing that we have ways of
being aware of ourselves that they don't have of being aware of us
doesn't take us beyond "our common world."

Nor does recognizing propositions incorporating these, and related, special forms of awareness as Millian modes of presentation.
Although doing so results in some propositions that some agents
can't *entertain,* it doesn't result in propositions impossible for them
to *cognize*—e.g., by making them subjects of predication—or to evaluate as true or false. Consider, for example, the proposition *that I am
in danger,* the entertainment of which requires identifying me in the
first-person way. Although only I can entertain it, other agents—
who are as familiar with predication and with the first-person mode
of presentation as I am—can think about it by thinking of me and
being in danger, and understanding how these elements interact in
the target proposition. Having done so, they can evaluate it as

having the same truth value as its representationally identical twin—
that SS is in danger—which they can entertain. All of the elements of
both propositions, as well as the propositions themselves, are constituents of our common world. The same can be said when other
Millian modes of presentation are in play.

The key point is that the inability to entertain a proposition p need
not be accompanied by the inability to entertain a proposition that
represents the world *exactly* as p does. This result doesn't hold for
Frege-Russell propositions. If one of those propositions could, in principle, be entertained only by me, then some constituent of it—some
object, concept, property, or sense—would be represented in a way
that no proposition entertainable by others represents it. Although
that, in turn, might well lead to the kind private perspectives that
Perry finds worrisome, no such worry arises for cognitive propositions. For every set of cognitive propositions some of which put constraints on agents capable of entertaining them, there is a corresponding set without those constraints from which it follows that things are
exactly as they are represented by the first system. In short, when
propositions are properly conceived as cognitive acts or operations,
the limited ability to entertain certain propositions poses no threat to
our common world. Because of this, there is no need to resort to an
extensive and (I believe) unjustifiable error theory involving belief
ascriptions and the explanation of action to account for our ordinary
thought and talk involving 'I', 'now', and other indexicals.

This is where I depart from Perry's otherwise insightful discussions. Although we both believe that uses of attitude ascriptions

5.   A asserts/believes/knows etc. that S.

standardly report an agent's cognitive state by specifying a relation—
assertion, belief, knowledge, etc.—the agent stands in to a proposition, Perry thinks that a large subclass of such cases *cannot* be

understood in this way. Rather, he thinks, they must be understood as reporting that the agent bears a somewhat different cognitive relation to something that isn't a proposition. This new element is a *belief state* which, although it determines a Russellian proposition, does so in a special way. For Perry, to understand attitude reports in this subclass as saying something true iff the agent A bears the standard assertion, belief, or knowledge relation to the proposition S is used to express is to render many of them false that we ordinarily take to be obviously true. So, on his picture, either we are systematically deceived, or we unconsciously impose nonstandard truth conditions—incorporating cognitive information not contained in the proposition—on a special subclass of attitude reports. Given cognitive propositions, we can see that this is a false choice; propositions incorporating the needed information about first-person and other modes of cognition are readily available.

The same points apply to the sophisticated theory of cognitive content presented in Perry (2001a, 2001b). Although that theory goes some way toward addressing the Problem 1 above for Perry (1977, 1979), Problems 2 and 3 remain. To repeat, being true to our pretheoretic attitude ascriptions while also being true to our use of these ascriptions in explaining actions requires recognizing pairs of propositions p and p* that differ only in that to entertain p* is to entertain p in a certain way, though p itself can be entertained in other ways as well. Perry cannot avail himself of such pairs or propositions. For him, my cases involving *propositions* p and p* are cases in which what he calls *the subject matter of two mental states* agree, but the truth conditions of *those states* differ.[14]

Here is a first-person example. Suppose I have amnesia and I am trying to figure out whether I am David Kaplan or Scott Soames,

[14] Perry (2001a), pp. 20–22, 68–69, 107, 113–15, 123, 132–33.

whom I know to be different philosophers. In considering one possibility, I predicate *not being DK* of myself, identified in the first-person way. On the cognitive propositions conception I thereby entertain two propositions—one that simply predicates *not being DK* of SS and one that requires SS to be identified in the first-person way. On Perry's account, I entertain only the former proposition. Later, I tentatively endorse my first-person predication, even though I am not confident enough to assertively utter, "I am not David Kaplan." According to the cognitive conception, I tentatively come to believe the second of the two propositions previously entertained (while continuing to be sure of the first), even though I am still not confident enough to assert what I now tentatively think. On Perry's story, there is no new proposition I come to believe, but there is something he calls "Scott's new belief."[15] It is my cognitive belief state, which contains a first-person representation denoting one who is in that state (in this case, me), as predication target of *not being DK* (which is represented by another part of the belief state). Though not a proposition, this belief state has truth conditions. It—or rather the state that consists of me being its agent—is true iff its agent, SS, isn't DK.[16] Since I wasn't in this state before, it is said to be a "new belief"—one I didn't have when I merely believed that SS wasn't DK.

That is Perry's basic picture. Here are a few generic worries. First, what are we to make of the extension of the story in which I come to know that I am not David Kaplan, and assertively utter (6)?

---

[15] For Perry's use of 'thought', 'belief', and 'knowledge' in this sense see Perry (2001a), pp. 20–21, 112, 115, 118, 122–23, 130–33.

[16] Note, these truth conditions of the state mention the state itself. For this reason Perry calls them *reflexive truth conditions*. They are part of what he calls *the reflexive content* of the state. The state also has propositional content, which is simply the proposition that SS isn't DK. See Perry (2001a), pp. 20–21, 122–33.

6. I now know, and hereby assert, something I previously didn't
know and wasn't willing to assert, namely (the proposition)
that I am not David Kaplan.

Although it seems obvious that this remark is perfectly true, on Perry's account it appears, strictly speaking, to be false. After all, on his
account there is no proposition I come to know that I didn't already
know, and no proposition I now assert that I wouldn't have willingly
asserted before. By contrast, the cognitive conception has no problem with the case. According to it, when I utter (6), I assert something both true and informative, while asserting nothing false.

Second, in addition to being problematic in itself, Perry's strategy
of speaking of new *thoughts* or *beliefs* even when no new propositions
are believed is not easy to generalize. One can see this by focusing on
attitude verbs—'question', 'doubt', 'deny', and 'learn'—that, unlike
'believe' and 'think', don't have nominalized forms that provide natural arguments of the truth predicate. Just as I can *believe* that *SS* is
such-and-such without believing that *I* am such-and-such, so I can
question, doubt, deny, or *learn* that *SS* is such-and-such without *ques-
tioning, doubting, denying,* or *learning* that *I* am such-and-such. In such
cases, we routinely speak of *what is questioned, doubted, denied, or
learned,* easily identifying its truth conditions—just as, in analogous
cases, we routinely speak of *what is believed,* identifying its truth
conditions.[17]

---

[17] All of these attitude verbs can take arguments of the form ⌜the proposition
that S⌝ in addition to bare tensed clauses ⌜that S⌝. However, many verbs v that can
take the latter can't take the former, even though we routinely talk of ⌜what is v-ed⌝
and of ⌜v-ing something⌝. Although the details of these constructions are daunting,
I take propositions to be central to the meanings of all of them. For me, a key distinction between verbs like 'believe', 'question', 'doubt', 'deny', and 'learn', which
take ⌜the proposition that S⌝, and those like 'think', 'hope', and 'expect' that take
⌜that S⌝ instead, is that the former are two-place predicates on agents and propositions, while the latter are operators the extensions of which map the propositions

According to the cognitive conception, *what is questioned, doubted,*
denied, or learned is *the proposition that SS is such-and-such*, the truth
conditions of which are those of its cognitively distinct but representationally identical counterpart, *the proposition that I am such-and-*
such. Thus, when my cognitive state changes, and I do come to question, doubt, deny, or learn *that I am such-and-such*, I come to bear the
relevant attitude to a proposition to which I hadn't born that attitude before, even though the new proposition is representationally
identical to one to which I did previously bear the attitude. This is
what is truly reported when I assertively utter (7).

7.   Only recently have I come to question (doubt, deny, or learn)
     that I am such-and-such.

What, on Perry's picture, is the truth reported by my utterance of
(7)? It can't be that I have only recently come to question (doubt,
deny, or learn) the proposition *that SS is such-and-such* because, by
hypothesis, I bore the relevant attitude or attitudes to it before. With
this in mind, compare truth of (7) with that of (8) in a case in which
I have long believed that SS is such-and-such.

8.   Only recently have I come to believe that I am such-and-such.

For Perry, the new *belief* that (8) reports is *not* a proposition newly
believed, but a belief state I had not been in before. Like all beliefs,
this one is, for Perry, true or false. Although this sounds natural, the
reason it does is that the nominal form 'belief' of 'believe' can be
used to refer to *what is believed* (aka the proposition believed). The
same can't be said for the verbs in (7). That is why we *don't* speak of

---

expressed by their sentential arguments onto one-place predicates of agents. This
difference does not, I think, affect the philosophical points above. Thus, verbs like
'think', 'hope', and 'expect' can be added to the list—'believe', 'question', 'doubt',
'deny', and 'learn'—used in this argument. I will return to this issue in chapter 11.

"*my question* that I am such-and-such," "*my doubt* that I am such-and-such," or "*my denial* that I am such-and-such" as being *true*, or *false* either. What is true or false is *what I questioned, doubted, or denied*, which is the first-person proposition the existence of which Perry denies. In the case of *learn*, there is no nominalized form of the verb at all. What is true or false is the first-person proposition I only recently learned.

The point can be applied to 'believe' itself. It is a commonplace that what is believed—*that I am such-and-such*—is something that may have been asserted, denied, doubted, learned, rejected, or merely imagined by me. *In short, the truth bearer that I believed is identical with one to which I can bear the other attitudes.* What is it, if not the first-person proposition Perry rejects? Although he identifies it with the mental state M such that for me to be in M is for me to believe *that SS is such-and-such* in the first-person way, presumably *that* isn't what I may also have asserted, questioned, denied, doubted, learned, rejected, or merely imagined. I don't assert, question, deny, doubt, learn, reject, or merely imagine my state of *believing*.[18] Nor, obviously, is it identical with any attitude state M* such that for me to have been in M* in the past, or at some possible world-state, was, or would have been, for me to assert, to question, to deny, to doubt, to learn, to reject, or merely to imagine *that I was such-and-such*.

These difficulties with Perry (2001a, 2001b) can be avoided, while leaving most of the many insights of those works intact, by adopting the cognitive conception of propositions. Since in other respects the cognitive paths he and I have been pursuing have much in common, it should be possible to bring our perspectives closer together.

---

[18] Rather, I bear these attitudes to the same thing that I bear the attitude of belief—a proposition believed rather than a state M of believing. For Perry, the state M of believing a certain proposition in a certain way is not itself a, or the, proposition believed by virtue of being in M.

MILLIAN SEMANTICS, FREGE'S PUZZLE, AND EXPANSIVE PRAGMATICS

I now broaden the discussion to include proper names and natural kind terms. Millian semantics takes the semantic contents of these terms to be the individuals or kinds they designate. To say this is to say that these designata are what those terms contribute to the propositions semantically expressed by sentences containing them. Thus, Millianism about these terms gives rise to classic versions of Frege's puzzle, including those in which 'Hesperus' is substituted for 'Phosphorus', or 'H_2O' is substituted for 'water', either in simple sentences or in the complement clauses of attitude ascriptions.

9a.   . . . Hesperus . . .
9b.   . . . Phosphorus . . .
10a. . . . water . . .
10b. . . . H_2O . . .
11a. John believes that . . . Hesperus . . .
11b. John believes that . . . Phosphorus . . .
12a. John believes that . . . water . . .
12b. John believes that . . . H_2O . . .

The burden of Millianism has been to explain how the (a) and (b) sentences can semantically express the same proposition— and so *mean the same thing*—despite differing so obviously in informativeness.

The first unequivocal defense of Millianism about names and natural kind terms, coupled with a well-worked-out formal semantic theory incorporating structured propositions, is found in Salmon (1986, 1989a, and 1990). On the view developed there, sentences semantically express Russellian propositions containing worldly constituents—objects, individuals, natural kinds, etc.—designated by proper names and natural kind terms. Just as one can fail to recognize a worldly item—e.g., Venus or water—on different occasions in which one encounters it, so one can fail to recognize a proposition containing it when one encounters that proposition on different occasions. Since our cognition of propositions is often mediated by sentences that express them, this can happen when one cognizes p, once via sentence (9a) or (10a) and once via (9b) or (10b). Semantics stipulates that ⌜x believes S⌝ is true at context C with A as agent iff S semantically expresses p at C and there is a *guise* by which p is presented to A (e.g., a sentence, or other cognitive or perceptual representation) to which A is disposed to inwardly assent. So if S and S* both semantically express p at C, then ⌜x believes S⌝ and ⌜x believes S*⌝ are either both true, or both false, of A at C.

Nevertheless, speakers who understand the language, while also knowing that Hesperus is Phosphorus and water is H_2O, are typically unaware of this and often wrongly think otherwise. According to Salmon, the reason for their error is that they make a false inference from the correct observation that a speaker reporting A's belief will naturally select a sentence S that not only expresses the proposition p that A is deemed to believe, but also suggests a guise similar to that to which A inwardly assents. So, when a speaker selects (11a)/ (12a) to report John's belief, rather than (11b)/(12b), a hearer will reasonably take the speaker to suggest that A would express the reported belief using (9a)/(10a), or something with similar associations. The error is in taking this pragmatic suggestion to be part of what is asserted, and of what the belief ascription means. It is not. For Salmon, the (a) and (b) ascriptions are synonymous, and are used to assert the same thing. In general, the pragmatic suggestions carried by uses of attitude ascriptions have no effect on the contents of the assertions (or other speech acts) they are used to make.

In retrospect, the chief strengths of this view were (i) its recognition (expressed using the term 'guises', adapted from Castaneda 1966, 1967, 1968) of the multitude of different linguistic and perceptual ways of believing, and bearing other attitudes to, propositions, (ii) its insistence that agents' awareness of these ways of entertaining propositions has an impact on the information communicated by uses of sentences containing names and natural kind terms, and (iii) its explanation of how and why the inclusion of worldly constituents in propositions inevitably leads to some situations in which agents fail to recognize different occurrences of the same proposition, fail to see the logical relationships between related propositions, and unknowingly accept contradictory propositions.[19]

The chief difficulties with the view are the massive errors it attributes to otherwise knowledgeable speakers involving assertions they make and beliefs they express using sentences they understand—which, in turn, are related to their unexplained ignorance of what those sentences mean. Why, if the meaning of a name (or the kind designated by a simple natural kind term) is its referent, don't those who know that Hesperus is Phosphorus (or that water is H_2O) also know that 'Hesperus' and 'Phosphorus' (or 'water' and 'H_2O') *mean the same thing*, and that the a and b sentences in (9*)–(12*) do too?

9*a.   Hesperus $\neq$ Hesperus.
9*b.   Hesperus $\neq$ Phosphorus.
10*a. Water isn't water.
10*b. Water isn't H_2O.
11*a. John asserted/believed that Hesperus $\neq$ Hesperus.
11*b. John asserted/believed that Hesperus $\neq$ Phosphorus.

---

[19] Kripke (1979) also made a very important contribution to establishing (iii).

12*a. John asserted/believed that water isn't water.

12*b. John asserted/believed that water isn't H_2O.

Why do speakers who understand the terms and know that Hesperus is Phosphorus and water is H_2O, remain firmly convinced that *it is possible for an agent to believe or assert* that Hesperus isn't Phosphorus or that water isn't H_2O (e.g., by accepting or assertively uttering (9*b)/(10*b)) without thereby *believing or asserting* that Hesperus isn't Hesperus or that water isn't water? Doesn't this suggest that the cognitive and assertive contents of uses of a sentence S, and of ascriptions ⌈A asserts/believes that S⌉ containing S, may depart significantly from the semantic content of S?

Soames (2002, 2005b) answers this last question in the affirmative, loosening the link between the meaning of a sentence and the contents of speech acts performed by uses of it. This, in turn, makes it possible to explain why certain sorts of ignorance of linguistic meaning should be expected of competent speakers, and so do not constitute objections of semantic Millianism. According to the view developed in these and later works, the semantic content of proper name or natural kind term N is merely the referent R of N. Nevertheless, uses of N often contribute a constituent consisting of R together with descriptive content associated with N in the context of utterance to the propositional contents of speech acts performed using N. Hence, assertions made and beliefs expressed by utterances of sentences containing N often go well beyond the semantic contents of those sentences.[20] For example, what is asserted by one who utters (9*b)/(10*b) is typically very different from what would be asserted by uttering (9*a)/(10*a). The same is true of the attitude ascriptions (11*a)/(12*a) vs. (11*b)/(12*b). This is particularly important in

---

[20] Soames (2002), chapter 3.

cases in which what is asserted by uttering (11*a)/(12*a) differs in truth value from what is asserted by uttering (11*b)/(12*b).[21]

Since utterances of sentences often result in multiple assertions, and even a nonindexical sentence S can be used to assert sharply different propositions in different contexts, the semantic content (meaning) of S is a *least common denominator* that remains constant across contexts.[22] This is not something to which individual speakers have, or could be expected to have, direct conscious access. Although competent speakers are reasonably good judges of *what they mean (assert)* by uses of sentences on various occasions, and hence of whether *they* would mean (assert) *the same thing* by utterances of *different* sentences on some occasion, this does not make them reliable judges about what is invariant in the information carried by uses of different sentences across all contexts for all users.[23] Thus, it is no embarrassment to semantic Millianism that its account of semantic content doesn't match speakers' intuitive judgments about linguistic meaning. What matters is that the semantic theory of the language can be combined with a plausible pragmatic account of assertion (and other speech acts) to accurately specify what speakers mean and assert by different uses of sentences.

The next two steps in the achievement of this goal are (i) the introduction of multiple Millian modes of presentation made possible by the cognitive conception of propositions, and (ii) the

---

[21] See Soames (2005b), and also Soames (2002), chapters 3, 6, and 8.

[22] In Soames (2002) this least common denominator is a proposition that is a necessary, obvious, and relevant consequence of the assertive content of S across all standard contexts. In Soames (2005b) it is a structured propositional matrix, different contextual completions of which yield the different propositions asserted by utterances of it in different standard contexts. Depending on the sentence and context of utterance, the proposition semantically expressed may or may not be among those asserted. There are even complete sentences the semantic contents of which are not complete propositions. For more on these complications, as well as defenses of the overall point of view, see Soames (2005b, 2006b, 2007b, 2010a).

[23] Soames (2002), pp. 68–72.

account, sketched in chapter 4, of what understanding an expression E consists in—beyond being able to use E to express the semantic content E_{SC} of E and (in some cases) to know of E_{SC} that it is the content of E. Together these two innovations widen the gap between *semantic content* and *assertive, speech, or other cognitive act content* by greatly extending the scope of pragmatic enrichment. Since Millian modes allow for enrichment without changing representational content, they allow us to avoid counterintuitive results about what is, or isn't, asserted, believed, or known, even in cases (illustrated in earlier chapters) in which descriptive enrichment that changes representational content is absent or severely limited. In other cases, Millian modes of presentation facilitate descriptive enrichment by providing elements already present in propositions asserted and believed that combine with information presupposed by conversational participants to generate descriptive enrichments (in the manner illustrated by examples (12)–(17) of chapter 4) that otherwise would be unavailable.

Finally, it should be noted that the account of understanding just sketched is based on a distinction between two senses of "meaning"— the semantic content of an expression E and the conditions that must be satisfied if a speaker is to be counted as understanding E—that generalizes and extends the distinction in Putnam (1970) between the *extension* of a natural kind term and the *stereotype* associated with it.[24] This distinction has, I believe, far greater importance than it has standardly been credited with. It is particularly useful when combined with theories of pragmatic enrichment of assertive and other speech act content.

---

[24] See in particular, the insightful discussion on pp. 148–52 of the reprinting of Putnam (1970) in volume 2 of his *Philosophical Papers*. For related discussion, see Putnam (1973, 1975).

DAVID LEWIS'S CLASSICAL DISCUSSION
OF *DE SE* ATTITUDES

Next I turn to David Lewis's "Attitudes *De Dicto and De Se*," which introduced the now common terminology. It was, and likely remains, the most influential work on the subject. Here is his statement of the issue.

> Consider . . . two gods. They . . . know every proposition that is true at their world. . . . Still . . . [n]either one knows which of the two he is. . . . One lives on top of the tallest mountain, and throws down manna; the other lives on top of the coldest mountain and throws down thunderbolts. Neither one knows whether he lives on the tallest mountain or on the coldest mountain, nor whether he throws manna or thunderbolts. Surely their predicament is possible. (The trouble might perhaps be that they have an equally perfect view of every part of their world, and hence cannot identify the perspectives from which they view it.) *But if it is possible to lack knowledge and not lack any propositional knowledge, then the lacked knowledge must not be propositional.* If the gods came to know which was which, they would know more than they do. But they wouldn't know more propositions. . . . Rather . . . [o]ne . . . would correctly self-ascribe the property of living on the tallest mountain.[25]

According to Lewis, both gods know that the manna-thrower M lives on the tallest mountain, and the thunderbolt-thrower T lives on the coldest mountain. Each also knows, of M, *that he lives on the tallest mountain*—i.e., each knows the singular proposition expressed

---

[25] Lewis (1979), at p. 139 of the 1983 reprinting, my emphasis. All citations will be to this reprinting.

by 'x lives on the tallest mountain' relative to an assignment of M to 'x'. The same is true of the singular proposition expressed by 'x lives on the coldest mountain' relative to an assignment of T to 'x'. Nevertheless, they seem to lack knowledge. If M or T were to say, "I don't know whether I live on the tallest/coldest mountain," we would judge him to have spoken truly. (Admittedly, this is next to impossible to imagine.) This suggests to Lewis that *there are some things they don't know.* Since there are no propositions they don't know, he concludes that not all knowledge is propositional; sometimes what is known is a property that one could correctly self-ascribe.

There are, however, challenges to be met. First, we need to strip the account of its anti-hyperintensionalism. The need to do so is illustrated by an example in which the property self-ascribed is necessarily empty. With this in mind, imagine John Perry shopping in the supermarket, when he looks up at two differently placed security mirrors and sincerely accepts (13).

13. I am nearer to him [demonstrating the man seen in mirror 1] than I am to him [demonstrating the man seen in mirror 2].

Since he is the man seen in both mirrors, he self-ascribes *being nearer to Perry than to Perry.* Because this property is necessarily empty, it is, on Lewis's conception of properties as functions from world-states to extensions, identical with the property expressed by $\lceil$ is F and is nearer to Perry than to Perry $\rceil$ for any F. Assuming that 'self-ascribes' distributes over conjunction, we get the result that anyone who self-ascribes *being nearer to Perry than Perry* thereby self-ascribes every property (and its negation). Since this is impossible, no one self-ascribes what Perry seems to self-ascribe in accepting (13). In short, anti-hyperintensionalism should be eliminated from Lewis's account of *de se attitudes.*

The case for this conclusion can be strengthened by noticing that John and Mary express *different beliefs* by sincerely uttering "I am in danger"—despite the fact that they self-ascribe the same property—namely, *being in danger*. How does this fit the idea that *de se* belief is the self-ascription of properties? Not too badly, if we add that an agent x who *self-ascribes* P also counts as *ascribing* P of *x* (but not conversely). Whereas both involve predicating P of x, the former requires *identifying the target of one's predication of P in the first-person way*, while that latter doesn't. It will then follow that, in addition to their *de se* beliefs, John and Mary also have different *de re* beliefs. This seems right, as does a converse case in which the amnesiac Rudolf Lingens and his friend Otto express the same (*de re*) belief when, after recovering his memory, Lingens sincerely says, "This book is about me," and Otto agrees, saying, "That book is about you." Innocent enough, this useful way of connecting *de se* with *de re* worsens the problems of Lewis's anti-hyperintensionalism—making it impossible for Lingens, prior to his epiphany, to coherently take himself *not to be Lingens*. Since doing that would involve both self-ascribing *not being Lingens* and believing the necessary falsehood *that Lingens isn't Lingens*, an anti-hyperintensionalist can't acknowledge the possibility that Lingens might wrongly believe *that he isn't Lingens*.[26] Thus, the neo-Lewisian should adopt a finer-grained theory of properties and propositions.

But this is only the beginning. The amnesiac Lingens, trapped in the Stanford Library, poses further problems. Although he believes, and even knows, all propositions he learned from reading, we

---

[26] Here the Lewisian assumptions are that when S is necessarily false, ⌜A believes that S⌝ is necessarily equivalent to ⌜A believes that S & P⌝ for every P. Since 'believe' distributes over conjunction, the truth of the former guarantees the truth of ⌜A believes that P⌝ *for every P*. Since it is impossible for any agent to simultaneously believe everything (and its negation), it must be impossible for ⌜A believes that S⌝ to be true when S is necessarily false.

naturally describe him as "not knowing that *he* is Lingens," and "not knowing that *he* is trapped in the Stanford Library." Which propositions are these? Not the propositions *that Lingens is Lingens* and *that Lingens is trapped in the Stanford Library*. Everyone knows the former and Lingens knows the latter from his reading. Despite this, Lewis rightly maintains, Lingens is in no position to self-ascribe *being Lingens* and *being in the Stanford Library*. However, Lewis can't handle the simple extensions of the case. In one of these, discussed in chapter 4, Lingens looks in the mirror and says, "That's (He is) me!", self-ascribing *being him* (demonstrating himself). Since this *is* the property *being Lingens*, the neo-Lewisian has no way of resisting the incorrect conclusion that after looking in the mirror Lingens *knows that he is Lingens*—prior to recovering his memory and being willing to say, "I am Lingens." As shown in chapter 4, this implausible connection can be resisted by introducing Millian modes of presentation.

We get the same result from the extension of the example, discussed in chapter 5, in which a fellow amnesiac Otto, who is reading the Lingens biography over Rudolf's shoulder, suddenly remembers who Rudolf is, and utters (14).

14. I have just realized your name is 'Rudolf'.

Although the neo-Lewisian has no way of accounting for the fact that Otto speaks truly, the account developed in chapter 5 does. Taking (15) to be the semantic content of (14), in the context, we enrich that bare singular proposition expressed by (i) requiring Otto to be cognized in the *first-person* way and (ii) requiring RL to be cognized either perceptually or via the second-person pronoun (which, of course, Otto and RL both understand).

15. Only just now has it been so that (λx [x realizes RL is named 'Rudolf'] Otto)

That's not all. As noted in chapter 5, the example can be extended still further to include a third amnesiac, Blotto, with the three characters reading their own copies of the book, when Otto's epiphany leads him to utter (16), addressing Blotto.

16. I just realized that he [pointing at RL] is named 'Rudolf'.

In sum, there is a general problem here to which the cognitive conception of propositions provides a solution that the neo-Lewisian does not.

Finally, it should be noted that I have so far written as if Lewis took the objects of *de se* beliefs to be properties and the objects of other beliefs to be propositions. He didn't. Desiring a unified analysis, while judging propositions not to be objects of *de se* beliefs, he took properties to be the objects of all beliefs. On this view, to believe, *de se*, that one is in danger is to self-ascribe *being in danger*, while to believe that the Earth moves is to self-ascribe *being such that the Earth moves* (a property everything has). This is unconvincing. Properties like *being in danger* are not true or false. Since one's *de se* belief that one is in danger may be true, and since one's belief is true iff what one believes is true, *being in danger* is not something one believes. The same point holds for all standard cases of *de se* beliefs.

Could Lewis's artificial properties, like *being such that the Earth moves*, play the role of propositions as primary bearers of truth or falsity and objects of the attitudes? Anyone who takes them to be must explain how they are generated, individuated, and cognitively accessed. The problem for a hyperintensionalist neo-Lewisian is that the most natural way of doing so is parasitic on the cognitive conception of propositions, or something like it. For me, negating a property *being so-and-so*, predication of which represents its target as *being so-and-so*, generates the property *not being so-and-so*, predication of which represents its target as *not being so-and-so*. Similar stories hold for conjoining and disjoining properties, generating (n − 1)-place properties from n-place properties, and forming complex properties in other ways. In each case, agents' access to complex properties is explained by operations they perform on more fundamental properties, while the complex properties themselves are individuated by the ways in which predication of them represents their targets, from which we read off their contributions to the truth conditions of propositions.

This idea is easily extended to include operations generating properties that are parasitic on already generated propositions. Operating on the proposition *that John loves Mary or Bill hates Mary*, agents can generate the property—λx *[John loves x or Bill hates x]*— predication of which represents its target as being one whom John loves or Bill hates. Taking the degenerate case of this operation in which no constituent is abstracted from the original proposition, we generate the property *being such that John loves Mary or Bill hates Mary*; predicating it of any target represents what the original proposition represents. When S expresses p, ⌈is such that S⌉ stands for the property predication of which represents what p represents (and nothing further). Since the individuation of, and our cognitive access to, the property are both parasitic on the already explained individuation of, and access to, the proposition, these properties don't raise explanatory problems.

How does the neo-Lewisian individuate and explain our cognitive access to the properties expressed by ⌈is such that S⌉ and ⌈is such that R⌉ for arbitrary S and R, without invoking propositional intermediaries? Well, how are the Earth and *moving* related to *being such that the Earth moves*? This property isn't the property that x instantiates iff the Earth *moves*. There is no unique property satisfying that condition, since *being such that the Earth moves and first-order arithmetic is incomplete* does too. It is not enough to say that the complex property is *a property* satisfying the condition, since different properties satisfying the condition are needed as objects of different hyperintensional attitudes. One could build formal structures—trees, tuples, sets of sets—out of simple properties and objects, *and stipulate their instantiation conditions.* But unless the structure and the conditions assigned can be shown to be nonarbitrary, intrinsic bearers of truth conditions, this will at most model the entities the neo-Lewisian needs, not provide them.

The more promising route is to go representational—maintaining (i) that *being such that the Earth moves/is round* is the property that represents the Earth as moving/being round (without representing anything further) because one who predicates it of anything represents the Earth that way, (ii) that *being such that the Earth moves or the Sun is hot* is the property that represents the Earth as moving or the Sun as being hot (and nothing further) because one who predicates it of anything does, and so on. Promising though this may sound, it leads to a question that the neo-Lewisian doesn't want to face. "Since predicating *moving* of the Earth represents it as moving, shouldn't we already have the proposition *that the Earth moves,* before reaching the property *being such that the Earth moves*?" The obvious answer is "Yes." This is just another way of motivating the cognitive account of propositions—which allows one to construct degenerate properties like *being such that the Earth moves* from propositions, rather than treating such properties as proposition substitutes.

To sum up, the theory of *de se* attitudes I have begun to sketch in this book makes use of Lewis's central insight that first-person self-ascription/self-predication is a special form of cognition, while avoiding the problems and limitations inherent both in his anti-hyperintensionality and in his substitution of properties for propositions as objects of the attitudes. When propositions are recognized to be purely representational acts, the self-predications that characterize *de se* attitudes fall out as subtypes of representationally identical *de re* predications, thereby both establishing the needed connection between *de se* and *de re* attitudes and generalizing to a broader class of purely representational subtypes. The fact that propositions are inherently representational allows us to analyze truth as accuracy in a certain kind of representation, and to take both *de se* and *de re* propositions to be primary bearers of truth conditions. Finally, the propositions needed to correctly account for problematic puzzle cases are natural pragmatic enrichments of the propositions semantically expressed by the sentences used in generating the cases.

KRIPKE'S SYMPATHETIC RECONSTRUCTION OF FREGE ON INDEXICALS

Although cognitive propositions are metaphysically very different from Fregean propositions, the treatment I have suggested of propositions asserted by uses of first-person and present-tense sentences, as well as of those containing other indexicals, has some similarities with the sympathetic reconstruction and modification, in Kripke (2008), of Frege's thoughts on these subjects, expressed in the following passages.[27]

> But are there not thoughts which are true today but false in six months' time? The thought, for example, that the tree there is covered with green leaves, will surely be false in six months' time. No, for it is not the same thought at all. The words 'this tree is covered with green leaves' are not sufficient by themselves for the utterance, the time of utterance is involved as well. Without the time-specification thus given we have not a

---

[27] Saul Kripke (2008).

complete thought, i.e. we have no thought at all. *Only a sentence with the time-specification filled out, a sentence complete in every respect, expresses a thought.* But this thought, if it is true, is true not only today or tomorrow but timelessly.[28]

If a time indication is conveyed by the present tense one must know when the sentence was uttered to grasp the thought correctly. *Therefore the time of utterance is part of the expression of the thought.* If someone wants to say today what he expressed yesterday using the word 'today', he will replace this word with 'yesterday'. Although the thought is the same, its verbal expression must be different in order that the change of sense which would otherwise be affected by the differing times of utterance may be cancelled out. *The case is the same with words like 'here' and 'there'. In all such cases the mere wording, as it can be preserved in writing, is not the complete expression of the thought; the knowledge of certain conditions accompanying the utterance, which are used as means of expressing the thought, is needed for us to grasp the thought correctly.* Pointing the finger, hand gestures, glances may belong here too. The same utterances containing the word 'I' in the mouths of different men will express different thoughts of which some may be true, others false.[29]

Here Frege suggests that present-tense sentences, and those containing indexicals, are incomplete. To express a thought they must be supplemented—sometimes by the time of utterance, sometimes by demonstrations, and sometimes by the speaker. It is as if times,

---

[28] Frege (1997), p. 343, my emphasis.
[29] Ibid., p. 332, my emphasis.

demonstrations, or speakers were added as extra nonlinguistic constituents to the words of sentences to yield *completed sentences,* the senses of which are always true, or always false.[30]

Kripke develops this idea by taking the words in sentences like (16a–c) to express senses determining concepts that map times t onto truth iff Scott is sick at t (for (a)), sick on the day of t (for (b)), or sick on the day before t (for (c)).

16a. Scott Soames is sick (now).
16b. Scott Soames is sick today.
16c. Scott Soames was sick yesterday.

'Now', 'today', and 'yesterday' designate, respectively, the identity function on times, the function mapping times to days in which they occur, and the function mapping times to the day before they occur. In each case, one constituent of the *completed sentence* is the time u_t of utterance, which *refers to itself* by virtue of expressing an *acquaintance-based sense* that determines u_t. This sense is a constituent of the thought expressed by the completed sentence (along with a sense that determines the function denoted by 'now', 'today', or 'yesterday'). Thus, the thoughts expressed are eternally true, or false, depending on whether I am sick (a) at u_t, (b) on the day of u_t, or, (c) on the day before that day.

This approach is extended to examples like (17).

17. I am sick. (said by Scott at u_t)

Here, the words require two completions: a time and a speaker. On the occasion imagined, the *completed sentence* contains the time u_t of utterance and the compound constituent 'I'-plus-Scott. The former refers to itself by virtue of expressing *the sense*—the same for all

---

[30] Frege is reconstructed in this way in Salmon (2002).

agents—that captures the way in which they are acquainted with u_t at u_t—and by virtue of which they could *never* be acquainted with any other time. The latter refers to me by virtue of expressing *the sense*, cognizable only by me, that captures the way in which I am (always and at all possible world-states) "internally" acquainted with myself, and by virtue of which I am never acquainted with anything else (at any time of any world-state). As a result, the thought expressed by the completed sentence is a timeless truth, or falsehood, that can be entertained only by me, and only at u_t.

Kripke doesn't say very much about what an acquaintance-based sense is, other than indicating that it is one we grasp by being cognitively acquainted with an object in a particularly close and revealing way. However, enough has been said to suggest a stark inversion of the usual Fregean picture. The "acquaintance-based sense" associated with an object o is identified as *whatever is involved in our being intimately acquainted with and focusing on o*. This contrasts with the usual Fregean picture in which "the object we have in mind, of which we predicate properties and relations," is identified as *whichever object happens to satisfy the (descriptive) sense we have immediately before our minds in entertaining the proposition*. With acquaintance-based senses, the object, in effect, determines the sense, rather than the other way around. Since modes of presentation—senses—are, for Frege, things we have immediately before our minds by virtue of which we are counted as having predication targets in mind, it is not easy to understand how this can be. Since Millian modes of presentation are ways of cognizing things *without themselves being cognized*, or being *before the mind*, they give rise to no similar worry.

Although Kripke might not find this contrast congenial, it cannot be avoided, if he wishes to maintain standard Fregean assumptions. Among those assumptions are (a) that the sense of any singular term must present at most one designatum with respect to any world-state, and (b) that attitude ascriptions report relations holding between individuals and propositions expressed by their content clauses. If these assumptions are maintained, (i)–(v) must also be accepted.

(i) In order for me to be able to use first-person content clauses to report, or speculate about, my past, future, or possible first-person beliefs, my special acquaintance-based sense of myself can't change along these parameters. There must be just one first-person sense used by me to think about myself at all times and in all possible circumstances.

(ii) In order for me to now be able to use present-tense clauses—or those containing 'now'—to report or speculate about any other actual or possible agent's special "present-tense (or 'now') thoughts," the special acquaintance-based sense now used to think about the present time must not change from agent to agent. There should be just one acquaintance-based, present-tense sense that all agents, actual and possible, use to think about this particular time. The same holds for every time.

(iii) In order for the truth value at a merely possible world-state w of a first-person, present-tense proposition that is actually about me and the present time t to depend, as it should, on what is going on with me at t,w, these acquaintance-based senses must rigidly present the same things at every world-state (and time).

(iv) The first-person sense that any actual or possible agent x uses to think about x must be different from that used by any other actual or possible agent. Similarly, the present-tense sense used by actual or possible agents to think about a time t at t must differ from the present-tense sense used by agents at any other time to think about that time.

(v)   The first-person and present-tense acquaintance senses can't
      be identical with any non-acquaintance-based senses, the
      grasp of which can be explained without appeal to the sense
      of acquaintance needed to explain an agent's grasp of "ac-
      quaintance senses."

Taken together, these doctrines are very implausible, as I think
Kripke recognizes. Since he doesn't endorse assumption (b) above,
he is not committed to (i), (ii), or (v), and would not, I think, accept
them all (in an overall reconstruction of Frege's project). But since
he doesn't have a positive proposal to replace assumption (b), he
doesn't provide us with a specific alternative. Since my purpose here
isn't to evaluate either Kripke's reconstruction of Frege, or the various features of Frege's own discussion of indexicals, this is no matter.[31] My aim in this section is to contrast the ways in which objects
and Millian modes of cognizing them figure in cognitive propositions with a broadly Fregean conception of modes of presentations.

For Frege, a "mode of presentation" of an object o is an abstract,
unchanging, nonlinguistic entity that somehow determines o independently of us, but which, when we cognize it, counts as our thinking of o. This model works well enough when the mode of presentation is a property (or propositional function) that is true of o and
only o. We can, after a fashion, "think of" an object as being so-
and-so by virtue of mediately predicating *being so-and-so* of such a
property (or propositional function). For this reason, I, like Frege,
countenance propositional constituents that descriptively determine
targets of what is defined in chapter 2 as indirect predication. *What
I don't do is force all predication into this mode, thereby excluding objects (occurring as predication targets) from propositions; nor do I treat*

---

[31] These tasks are taken up in Soames (2014b), chapter 2, section 7.

all propositionally encoded ways of cognizing predication targets as prop-
ositional constituents, which are themselves objects of cognition. It is
because Frege does these things that it is so difficult for him to accommodate the first-person, present-tense, and indexical cases
generally.

For me, propositionally encoded first-person, present-tense, perceptual, linguistic, and recognitional *ways of cognizing predication
targets* are *ways we do certain things* (e.g., identify predication targets), not entities we immediately cognize in order to indirectly cognize objects those directly present entities supposedly determine on
their own. For this reason there is no need to posit a different form
of first-person cognition for each agent, or a different mode of
present-tense cognition for each moment of time (in the manner of
(iv)). On the contrary, since the different agents and moments of
time are themselves constituents of the relevant propositions, the
first-person and present-tense manners in which the propositions require these agents or moments to be identified (by those who entertain the propositions) may be the same, rather than differing from
agent to agent and moment to moment. Moreover, since the special
forms of first-person, present-tense, perceptual, linguistic, and recognitional cognition are not expected to themselves determine predication targets (independent of who is doing the cognizing, when the
cognition is occurring, what is causing the perceptual experience,
what antecedent facts have determined the referent of a name, or
what item is recognized as recurring), there is no need to guarantee
their rigidity in the manner of (iii). (After all, the objects are already
in the proposition.) Finally, since entertaining a proposition containing a restriction on how things are cognized counts as simultaneously entertaining a distinct but representationally identical proposition that lacks it, the fact that some cognitive perspectives are not
available to some agents at some times doesn't limit the ability of

those agents to represent the world, or even to represent the propositional attitudes of other agents, up to representational identity.

FREGE, KAPLAN, AND KRIPKE'S
"THE FIRST PERSON"

I will close this chapter with a few words about Kripke's discussion of the first person, the present tense, and related temporal indexicals in section 1 of Kripke (2011a). Though there is much there with which I agree, some insightful observations are intermingled with points that seem not quite right, but which can be set right by making use of the framework developed here. One passage illustrating this raises a question about the adequacy of Kaplan's semantic rule for the first-person singular pronoun—which we may take to tell us that *uses of the first-person singular pronoun by any speaker x directly refer to x*.[32] Asking whether this rule gives us a complete semantic description, Kripke says:

> What else could be needed? Well, recall my remarks that the [semantic] 'description from above' [provided without using indexicals in the rule] ought to be usable as an instruction manual for someone wishing to learn the language. Though Kaplan's explanation is all very well for some sort of descriptive anthropologist who may in fact have the concept of 'I', it would be very difficult to get it across to Frege (or anyone else who is presumed to lack the concept). So, for example, let Kaplan say to Frege. . . . "If any person S speaking German attributes a property using the word 'ich', then what S says or thinks is true iff S has that property." But how can Frege use

[32] I assume both that for an expression to directly refer to something is for that referent to exhaust its semantic content and that there is a way of spelling this out that is graspable by speakers.

the word 'ich' on the basis of these instructions? Should he think, "*Hmm*, so how am *I* going to use the word 'ich' on the basis of this general statement? Well, any German should attribute, say, being in pain or being a logician to *himself*, if and only if the German is in pain, or is a logician, as Kaplan says. So, *I* should do this." . . . [This] formulation would presuppose that Frege already has the concept of *himself*, the concept he expresses using 'ich'. So here we really are going in a circle.

The point is that each one of us speaks a language that he himself has learned. Each one of us can fix the reference of the word 'I' by acquaintance with oneself, self-acquaintance. There is no requirement that this type of acquaintance is given to us by a [purely] qualitative description expressible in a 'scientific language' spoken by no one [the kind of metalanguage Kripke takes Kaplan to aim at for his semantics of indexicals]. . . . No one can grasp the rule for 'I' stated in the common language except by means of one's own self-acquaintance. Otherwise, there would be no way of learning how the rule tells us to refer.[33]

There are two main insights here.

(i) Each person x is acquainted with x in a way no one else is, and so has a special, first-person way of thinking about, predicating properties of, and referring to x that others can't use to think about or refer to x.

(ii) Mastery of Kaplan's rule for 'I' (or any similar rule) isn't responsible for the ability in (i). Rather, it is only by using one's first-person way of thinking that one might find Kaplan's rule helpful in learning to use 'I' correctly.

[33] Kripke (2011a), 300–301.

Since these points were independently made in chapter 3, I won't further elaborate them here other than to agree with Kripke that they provide some vindication for Frege's remark that "everyone is presented to himself in a special and primitive way, in which he is presented to no one else."[34]

However, other aspects of the passage and the surrounding context are worrisome. For example, Kripke seems to suggest that Kaplan's semantics for 'I' leaves out something crucial. The third sentence of the passage is supposed to indicate what. "Well, recall my remarks that the [semantic] 'description from above' ought to be usable as an instruction manual for someone wishing to learn the language." The remarks we are invited to recall are these.

> What is a description 'from above'? . . . The description, first
> and foremost, is a description of how the language is used, but
> it also has an instructional aspect. If language can be described
> completely and correctly 'from above', in a neutral indexical-
> free language, the description (of, say, English) should be us-
> able as an *instruction* manual, a set of imperatives for a for-
> eigner wishing to learn English.[35]

Kripke suggests that Kaplan's semantic rule of 'I' is inadequate because it can't be used as an instruction for learning to use the word. But it can be so used. As noted in chapter 3, an agent A learning English who is given Kaplan's rule and wishes to use 'I' in accord with it will know, in the first-person way, when A is using 'I' with that intention. Hence, A will use it in self-ascribing properties A believes, in the first-person way, that A has. Since A knows that others are acquainted with themselves in the same first-person way that A

---

[34] Frege (1997), p. 333.
[35] Kripke (2011a), p. 294.

is acquainted with A, A will rightly take other English speakers to do the same. In short, A will understand, and be able to correctly use, the first-person singular pronoun.

Of course, A wouldn't arrive at this position if A didn't, at the outset, have the ability to think of A in the first-person way, and hence to have first-person thoughts. Kripke seizes on this in the initial passage. But why is it relevant? If it is to be a criticism of Kaplan, the idea must be that no rule R for the first-person singular pronoun is *properly* instructional, and hence *semantically* adequate, unless one who lacked the ability to think of oneself in the first-person way, and so lacked the ability to have first-person thoughts, could acquire those abilities by learning R.

But that can't be right. If it were, there could be no adequate semantic rule for the first-person pronoun, because the ability to think of oneself in the first-person way doesn't, and couldn't, come from mastering linguistic rules. Nor could there be an adequate semantic rule for any other word. Following any rule whatsoever— for baking a cake, assembling a bookcase, or using a word— requires the ability to monitor, in a first-person way not given by the rule, what one is doing. So, for any rule to guide my use of a word, I must have the ability to recognize, in the first-person way, when and how *I* am using that word. It would be absurd to conclude from this that no purported semantic rule for any word can be adequate. But if the only precondition required in order for Kaplan's rule for 'I' to be capable of guiding one's use of the word is equally a precondition for any rule to guide one's behavior, then there is no sense in which Kaplan's rule is objectionably incomplete or inadequate.

Next notice Kripke's use of the term 'concept' in the long passage quoted.

Though Kaplan's explanation is all very well for some sort of descriptive anthropologist who may in fact have *the concept of 'I'*, it would be very difficult to get it across to Frege (or anyone else who is presumed to lack *the concept*) [*my emphasis*]. . . . [This] formulation [in which Frege uses his first-person thoughts of himself together with Kaplan's rule to guide his use of the pronoun] would presuppose that Frege already has the concept of *himself*, the concept he expresses using 'ich'. So here we really are going in a circle.

What is a concept? Presumably it is something predicated (and hence true or false) of other things. I take it that concepts, in the sense that Kripke is using the term, are identical when predicating them of an item represents that item as being the same way. For each x, there is, I imagine, the concept *being x*. Is there some other concept, *being x him/her/itself*? No. There is no difference between representing something as (being) x and representing it as (being) x itself. The difference wrongly described as a difference in concepts is the difference between two ways of predicating the same concept— between predicating *being x* and predicating *being x*, identifying the predication target, x, in the first-person way. Just as *a person x* and *a person x identified in a certain way* are not different persons, so a concept predicated one way and a concept predicated another way are not different concepts. Given the cognitive conception of propositions, we incorporate the two different acts of predication of the same concept into representationally identical but cognitively distinct propositions. It is true that Kaplan's failure to recognize such propositions is a serious shortcoming in his philosophy of language. But this doesn't show his semantic rule for 'I' to have *left out any concept*, or even to be *incomplete*. All his rule requires is what must to be added to any semantic theory—namely, the cognitive conception of propositions plus a philosophy of mind that recognizes first-person cognition. Given these plus Kaplan's semantic rule for 'I', it is predictable that speakers will use sentences containing 'I' to express first-person thoughts.

The point about concepts is connected to another problem having to do with Kripke's defense of Frege. For each agent x, Frege was looking for what I would call a 'concept' (but he would call a 'sense') that (i) was uniquely true of (or uniquely determined) x, and (ii) only x could grasp. This concept/sense was to be a constituent of x's first-person thoughts, i.e., of Fregean propositions that only x could entertain. Since objects are never constituents of Fregean propositions, he required, for each agent x, a purely qualitative sense, graspable only by x, that uniquely determines x. Both Perry (1977) and Kaplan (1989) criticize Frege for imposing this impossible demand on agents. Although Kripke rightly recognizes the demand to be impossible in the following excerpt from the original passage, he wrongly rejects the idea that Frege needed to impose it in the passage just below it:

> Each one of us can fix the reference of the word 'I' by acquaintance with oneself, self-acquaintance. There is no requirement that this type of acquaintance is given to us by a [purely] qualitative description expressible in a 'scientific language' spoken by no one.[36]

> There is no difficulty for Frege . . . once we rid ourselves of the idea of a 'scientific language' spoken by no one. . . . Each of them [each agent x] could determine the referent [of x's use of 'I'] by his own acquaintance with himself.[37]

---

[36] Ibid., p. 301.
[37] Ibid., p. 300.

Here, Kripke is thinking of the analysis in Kripke (2008) discussed in the previous section. According to that analysis, each agent A is acquainted with A in a special way that no one else is acquainted with A, and this acquaintance provides A with a Fregean sense that uniquely determines A. Here, Kripke ignores (i) the argument just given that the nature of Fregean propositions requires all senses to be purely qualitative; (ii) the difficulties, rightly emphasized by Perry and Kaplan, in understanding how different agents with qualitatively identical mental lives could have different Fregean senses before their minds; and (iii) the other criticisms of Kripke (2008) mentioned in the previous section. He also ignores the way in which all these difficulties can be avoided by (a) dispensing with Fregean *acquaintance-based senses* and allowing agents themselves to occur as constituents of propositions, and (b) allowing their first-person ways of cognizing themselves to occur as Millian modes of presentation in cognitive propositions that don't affect representational contents of those propositions.[38]

---

[38] Analogous points apply to the brief discussion on p. 303 of Kripke (2011a) of a broadly Fregean way of treating propositions expressed by uses of sentences containing 'now' and 'today'.

Overcoming Objections

In chapter 1, I explained the need for new foundations in the study of language, mind, and information. Included were (i) the need to more sharply distinguish the information semantically encoded by a sentence from the assertions it is used to make and the beliefs it is used to express in different contexts, (ii) the need to distinguish what *understanding* an expression E consists in (which comes in degrees) from knowing of the representational content of E that it is the content of E, and (iii) the need to develop a conception of propositions as pieces of information capable of (a) solving the metaphysical and epistemological problems that have defeated traditional conceptions of propositions while (b) recognizing the distinct but related demands that real propositions place on the world they represent and the minds that entertain them.

The core of this project is the conception of propositions as purely representational cognitive acts presented in chapter 2, which emphasized the solution to the foundational problems mentioned in (iiia). Addressing them involved solving the traditional problem of the unity of the proposition, explaining how an organism without the concept of a proposition, or the ability to cognize one, can know or believe propositions, and further explaining how sophisticated agents can acquire the concept, and come to know things about propositions, by monitoring their own cognitions. Further progress was made by explaining what it is for a (nonindexical) sentence S to mean p in L. According to the cognitive conception, it is for speakers of L to use S to perform p. For example, one who understands the sentence 'The Union Jack is a symbol of Britain' uses the name to pick out the flag and the verb phrase to predicate *being a symbol of Britain* of it. Since to do this is *to perform* the act that is the proposition expressed, one's use of the sentence is one's entertaining the proposition. Since no other cognition is needed, learning that S means p in L doesn't require learning that S stands in some theoretically specified relation R to p.

Chapter 2 also laid the basis for the conception of representationally identical but cognitively distinct propositions needed to implement the goal (iiib) of recognizing the distinct but related demands that propositions place on the world they represent and the minds that bear attitudes to them. Chapters 3–8 implemented this conception in some detail, while using the cognitive conception to more carefully distinguish the information semantically encoded by a sentence from the assertions it is used to make and the beliefs it is used to express, and to prize apart *understanding* an expression E from knowing of the representational content of E that it is the content of E. The end results were, I hope, the beginnings of new solutions to contemporary problems in semantics, the philosophy language and the philosophy of mind.

Having done that, I now turn to objections to the cognitive conception. The first, and most common objection, was voiced in chapter 2—namely, that propositions can't be acts because they aren't things we do. *To think otherwise is to make a category mistake.* Nor, the objection continues, would it help to identify propositions with event types, which occur or happen. Just as it sounds bizarre to say that the proposition that $3^2 + 4^2 = 5^2$ is something I have often done, so it sounds bizarre to say that it has often happened. Thus, it is plausible to suppose that if one of these identifications is refuted by ordinary "intuition," the other is too. In this chapter, I will argue that neither are.

Consider, to begin with, a version of the Frege-Russell conception of number. Zero is the set whose only member is the empty set; one is the set of those sets z that contain some x, and only x, as a member; two is the set of sets z that contain some distinct x and y, and only x and y, as members; and so on. The successor of a set n is the set of sets z such that removing a member of z yields a member of n. A natural number is a member of the smallest set containing zero and closed under successor. The conception was brilliant and the methodology was sound—numbers are whatever they must be to explain our arithmetical knowledge. Had that explanatory goal been met, no one would have objected that the Frege-Russell conception can't be right because it violates our "intuition" that people are not members of members of numbers.

Just as the explanatory standard was correct for numbers, so it is also correct for propositions. In both cases, we know many facts about the target entities while knowing next to nothing about the kinds of things they are. We have no images of numbers or propositions and no robust pretheoretic sense of what they are. If asked to pick out the entity that is the number 7 or the proposition that the Sun is a star, common sense draws a blank. Since most candidate entities appear to be nonstarters, the search for explanation is all we have. The crucial difference between the two cases is that we *can* give good explanations of the relations we bear to propositions, the knowledge we have of, or about, them, and their ability to do the work we require of them.

In chapter 2, I explained the cognitive conception's *foundational* advantages. Its advantages for theory construction are no less important. Here, the contrast with Frege-Russell numbers is stark. Whereas the established theorems of arithmetic didn't depend on, but rather provided a crucial test for, that conception, empirical theories in which propositions figure aren't independent of the cognitive conception. Fragmentary, conceptually incomplete, and subject to revision, these theories yield different results when combined with different conceptions of propositions. By supplying us with representationally identical but cognitively distinct propositions, the cognitive conception delivers results we need. Because these propositions represent the same things as being the same ways, they impose identical truth conditions on the world. Because they are cognitively distinct, they impose different conditions on minds that entertain them. As argued in chapters 3–8, this opens up many new opportunities for explaining cognitive and linguistic facts.

In all those cases, conceiving of propositions as purely representational cognitive acts facilitates the derivation of correct but otherwise elusive results about what is believed, asserted, and so on. These results extend the naturalistic epistemology of propositions that began with a story of how one can know, assert, and believe them by cognizing, not propositions themselves, but the objects and properties that are their subject matter. That story continued with an account of how self-conscious agents acquire knowledge of them by attending to events in their cognitive lives. Once identified, propositions are made targets of predications, enabling agents to entertain various complex propositions, including propositional attitude ascriptions. This was the basis of the explanations given in chapters 3–8 of attitudes born to propositions incorporating Millian modes of presentation, and to propositions that ascribe attitudes incorporating those modes. All that was required by these explanations was for agents to have the ability to identify predication targets via these Millian modes, and for them to have the concepts on which those modes are based.

That, in sum, is how taking propositions to be purely representational cognitive acts allows us to explain our knowledge of, and the relations we bear to, propositions. Why then does it initially seem absurd to say that propositions are things we do? The answer is not far to seek. If one asks oneself, pretheoretically, "What is a proposition?" one naturally starts with examples. What is the proposition *that arithmetic is reducible to set theory, that it is sunny in Seattle,* or *that there is a red dot on the otherwise blank wall in front of me*? In bringing these examples to mind, one thinks of arithmetic, set theory, Seattle, and the wall as being certain ways. One doesn't necessarily judge them to be those ways, one merely entertains the propositions that they are. In some cases one may also conjure up images, but even then one knows that the proposition entertained isn't the image in one's mind, but something more general.

There is, however, something in the visual model to which we wrongly tend to cling. Just as *seeing* a wall with a red dot is a phenomenally robust form of *being aware of* it, so, we are incautiously inclined to think, *visualizing* the wall is a phenomenally poorer form of *awareness* of a mental image, while *entertaining* a proposition about the wall is a minimal, or even phenomenally empty, form of *awareness* of *something that represents the wall as being a certain way.* It isn't. To entertain a proposition is not to be aware of it, nor is to believe it to affirm something of which we are aware.

We are wrongly encouraged to think otherwise by the parallels, (i) and (ii), between our talk about perception and our talk about propositional attitudes.

(i)   Just as 'see' is a two-place predicate relating cognizers to things seen, so 'entertain', 'believe', 'assert', and 'know' are two-place predicates relating them to propositions entertained, believed, asserted, and known.

(ii) Just as standing in the relation expressed by 'see' requires cognizers to be aware of things involved in the perception, so standing in the relations expressed by 'entertain', 'occurrently believe', 'assert', and 'know' requires them to be aware of things involved in the attitudes.

The natural, but readily explainable, error is to jump from (i) and (ii) to (iii), when in fact it is (iv), rather than (iii), that is true.

(iii) Just as standing in the relation expressed by 'see' requires one to be aware of *the things seen*, so standing in the relation expressed by 'entertain', 'occurrently believe', 'assert', or 'know' requires one to be aware of *the propositions entertained, occurrently believed, asserted, or known*.

(iv) Although standing in the relation expressed by 'see' to *an object o that is seen* requires one to be aware of *o*, standing in the relation expressed by 'entertain', 'occurrently believe', 'assert', or 'know' to *a proposition p* merely requires one to be aware of the things p represents and the ways p represents them to be.

The error of opting for (iii) rather than (iv) is a main source of the incorrect idea that propositions can't be cognitive acts. Everyone knows one can *perform an act* without making *it* the object of one's awareness. Everyone also knows that forming or activating already formed cognitive and behavioral dispositions consequent on performing an act needn't involve thinking of the act. Since this is what entertaining and believing propositions amount to if propositions are cognitive acts, the objector's commitment to (iii) leads him to conclude that the cognitive conception is absurd. But it isn't absurd; (iii) isn't sacrosanct. It is no more intuitively plausible than (iv)—which receives crucial support from its role in solving the foundational problems of propositions and providing our cognitive and linguistic theories with entities they need.

Although this addresses a familiar objection, it also leaves us with a question. When agents become aware of propositions, first by entertaining and then by predicating properties of them, why do they remain unaware that propositions are cognitive acts? Why does one who entertains the proposition that Seattle is sunny, and predicates *being widely disbelieved* of it, fail to realize the kind of entity it is? Since ordinary human agents, who do make propositions objects of thought in this way, don't have any precise idea of what they are, every theorist faces this question.

Here is my answer. Suppose an agent entertains the proposition that Seattle is sunny and focuses on the event token which is his entertaining of it. This token isn't what he takes to be widely disbelieved. Rather, he would say, *that type of thing* is widely disbelieved. What type? Is it the *event type* in which one predicates being sunny of Seattle, is it the *act type* performance of which results in an event of that type, or is it some other type? It is, in fact, whatever type best plays the proposition role in our theories—which, I have maintained, is the repeatable act type of predicating *being sunny* of Seattle. But this philosophical answer isn't one an ordinary agent would give. All the agent can say about the type (i.e., proposition) is that it is *the thought he just had*—which is true enough provided he doesn't succumb to the *seeing-in-the-mind's-eye* temptation of taking the thought to be both (i) what he focused on when whispering "Seattle is sunny" to himself and (ii) what he always focuses on when "thinking that thought."

If he does succumb, he is likely to object when told that the thought he entertained when whispering to himself was his act of entertaining it—which it must be if propositions are cognitive acts. The agent who has succumbed to the *mind's-eye* temptation will object because he wrongly thinks that entertaining a thought (always) involves focusing on *it*. Thinking this, he may protest, "Obviously *what I was focusing on* when I whispered 'Seattle is sunny' wasn't *my act of focusing on it*." To which we respond: *Of course, there was no single act which was both what you focused on and your focusing on it. You performed two different acts at once. Just as you can perform a physical act while cognitively focusing on what you are doing, so you can perform one cognitive act while simultaneously performing a second act which involves focusing on the first.* What you focused on when entertaining the proposition that Seattle is sunny was Seattle, which isn't an act. But if, in response to our question *What is that proposition?*, you self-consciously attended to *what you were doing* while you were doing it, then you *did*, in addition, focus on the act of predicating *being sunny* of Seattle. You performed two cognitive acts at once. One was the act of predicating *being sunny of Seattle*—which is the proposition that Seattle is sunny; the other was your focusing on that act while performing it. Your error was in conflating those two acts into an imagined single act of *entertaining x by focusing on x*. Rightly rejecting that as absurd, you wrongly rejected the idea that the proposition entertained wasn't the act of predicating *being sunny* of Seattle. Eliminating the *mind's-eye* temptation eliminates that objection. With this we explain both how unsophisticated agents can bear attitudes to propositions without being able to cognize them and how self-conscious agents succeed in identifying them. We also identify and correct the errors responsible for the spurious "intuition" that propositions can't be things we do.

Next, I turn to a related objection that rests on three claims: (i) cognitive acts can't be propositions if they can't be true or false; (ii) cognitive acts can't be true or false, if they don't represent things as being certain ways; (iii) to represent things as being certain ways is *to do something*, which *acts of representing* can no more do than acts in general can do what their agents do in performing them. The first claim of this trio is true, but the conjunction of the second and third isn't. Let's begin with the third, which is based on the observation that it doesn't, in general, follow from the fact that *an agent does so-and-so* that *his act does so-and-so.* On the face of it, nothing could be more obvious. From the fact that John admires Mary, it doesn't follow that the act *admiring Mary* itself admires Mary. Still, we do sometimes ascribe properties to acts that *derive from* the properties of agents who perform them.

For example, we say that an act is insulting when for one to perform it is for one to insult someone; we say that it is irresponsible when to perform it is to neglect one's responsibilities. In saying this, we are not saying that the act type itself does anything to cause offense or that it has been remiss in fulfilling its obligations. Since an act neither *does* anything in the sense an agent does, nor has any responsibilities, the sense in which an act may be insulting or irresponsible is not the same as the sense in which an agent who performs it insults or is irresponsible. When one says, referring to an act, "That was an irresponsible thing to do," what one says is true iff it is possible to accurately describe the agent as doing something—e.g., as making a promise with no intention of keeping it in such-and-such circumstances—from which it follows that the agent acts irresponsibly. Taking act types to be fine-grained—in the sense in which traveling to work is distinct from driving there (because to perform the latter is also to perform the former but not conversely)—we may characterize irresponsible acts as those every possible performance of which involves neglecting one's responsibilities. By parity of reasoning, a cognitive act type represents o as P iff every possible performance of it is one in which an agent represents o as P.

This brings us to the second claim of our trio. Is this derivative sense in which cognitive acts are representational sufficient to endow them with truth conditions? The idea that truth is a form of accuracy suggests that it is. In addition to assessing an agent's overall accuracy on various matters, we also need to assess the accuracy of the agent's sayings or cognitions, one by one. For this, we need truth and falsity, plus cognitive doings that *represent* things as being various ways, *where the sense in which they represent is derived from the sense in which agents do.* When to perceive or think of o as P is to represent o as it is, we identify an entity—a particular sort of perceiving or thinking—plus a property that entity has when this sort of perceiving or thinking is accurate. The entity is a proposition, which is the cognitive act of representing o as P. The property is truth, which the act has iff to perform it is for one to represent o as o really is. This derived sense of representation is all we need to accomplish the tasks for which we need the notions of truth and falsity.

The two objections I have dealt with thus far are, I think, common misconceptions masquerading as sacrosanct "intuitions." As I mentioned in chapter 2, they aren't the only such objections to current theories of propositions. There I cited an argument given by Richard Cartwright purporting to show that although many theorists regard propositions as *meanings* (in one important sense) of some nonindexical sentences, the idea that they are is absurd. The ordinary-language argument to this effect is based on a contrast between the pairs in (1) and (2).

1a. Bill   asserted/proved/contradicted/supported/questioned/ withdrew the proposition that arithmetic is reducible to logic.

1b. *Bill asserted/proved/contradicted/supported/questioned/ withdrew the meaning of the sentence 'Arithmetic is reducible to logic'.

2a. The proposition that arithmetic is reducible to logic is plausible/probable/untrue.

2b. *The meaning of the sentence 'Arithmetic is reducible to logic' is plausible/ probable/untrue.

Whereas the (a) examples are fine, the (b) examples sound bizarre, which encourages some to think they are category mistakes. They aren't. Like the objection to propositions as cognitive acts, this objection to propositions as meanings is based on a misleading pattern of ordinary talk.

In the case of meaning, this misleading pattern mixes two different realities. One is *semantic content*, which, with a sentence of a certain sort, is the information it semantically encodes. The other reality, touched on in chapter 4, is what is involved in *understanding* or *knowing the meaning* of a sentence or expression. This second reality—which must be distinguished from knowing of the semantic content of S or E that it is the content of S or E—involves having background knowledge plus inferential and recognitional abilities widely presupposed by other users, and so necessary for effective communication with them. Good theories should separate the two realities, while keeping propositions as cognitive acts that are semantic contents of some sentences, despite misleading ordinary-language arguments to the contrary.

Recognizing this helps us deal with a closely related objection—namely, that propositions aren't ever sentence meanings (semantic contents) because the predicate 'means' in 'S means that so-and-so' doesn't take noun phrase objects such as *the proposition that so-and-so*. This is illustrated by the fact that we don't say (3a), but do say (3b).

3a. *The sentence 'El libro es rojo' means the proposition that the book is red.

3b. The sentence 'El libro es rojo' means that the book is red.

The observation about the grammar of 'means' on which this objection is based is correct, but it doesn't show that propositions aren't meanings (in the sense of semantic contents) of some sentences. What it does show is that 'means' is not a *two-place predicate* relating expressions to their meanings (semantic contents). Nevertheless, the proposition *that so-and-so* may still be crucial to the semantics of the sentence *S means that so-and-so*. It will be crucial if, as I suspect, 'means' is an operator the extension of which maps the proposition p that is the semantic content of its complement clause onto the property *having (expressing) that semantic content*. On this picture, the proposition *that S means that the book is red* predicates the property *semantically expressing that content—i.e., that proposition*—of S.

Though this is the crux of the matter, there are further issues worth noting. First, in addition to *that*-clauses, 'means' also takes *wh*-expressions, as in *Jon knows what expression E means*. As we have already seen, *knowing what E means* tracks *understanding* E, which can't be identified with knowing anything in particular about E's semantic content. Second, we do have a noun phrase, *the meaning of E*. There is nothing grammatically incorrect about saying *the meaning of a name is the object it designates*, or *the meaning of a sentence is the proposition it semantically expresses*. If we wish *these sentences* to express truths, we must identify the meanings of names and sentences with their semantic contents. The case of the grammatically unobjectionable sentence *Jon knows the meaning of expression E* is more complicated. We use this sentence to say of John that he understands E, where to understand E is both to be able to use it with its semantic content and to have the knowledge and recognitional abilities widely presupposed by users of E, and so needed for effective communication with them. Although this interpretation of our pretheoretic *meaning talk* is complicated, something along these lines is, I think, needed if we are ever to have a scientific semantics.

The final objection to be dealt with has been pressed by Peter Hanks. He objects that it is incoherent to suppose, as I do, that acts of predication have truth conditions, if they are *forceless*, and so do not *commit* agents who perform them to an object's *having* the predicated property. Consider my distinction between *entertaining* the proposition that o is so-and-so and *judging* that o is so-and-so. To entertain the proposition is to predicate *being so-and-so* of o, and thereby to represent o as being so-and-so—which one does when one perceives, conceives, cognizes, or imagines o as being that way. Since in some of these cases my predication is forceless, the act of predication that is common to all of them does not committing me to o's being so-and-so. Commitment does enter when I *judge* o to be so-and-so. To judge is to predicate the property of o in an affirmative manner, which involves forming, or activating already formed, dispositions to act, both cognitively and behaviorally, toward o in ways conditioned by one's attitudes toward things that are so-and-so. Although this requires analytically distinguishing the acts of entertaining and judging that o is so-and-so, it doesn't require thinking of them as performed in sequence any more than the distinguishable acts of stirring the pot and carefully stirring the pot must be performed in sequence.

Now consider the act of *forcelessly predicating* being so-and-so of o, which is simply the noncommittal act of entertaining the proposition that o is so-and-so. Since for any act A, the act of performing A is identical to A itself, the act of performing a proposition p is identical to p. Since the act *entertaining p* is the act *performing p*, p itself is a noncommittal act. This is what we want. If propositions are to be acts, they must be noncommittal, in the sense of acts that have truth conditions but don't have correctness conditions. Thus, whereas it is perfectly natural to speak of tautologies as being true and their negations as being untrue, we don't generally speak of tautologies as being correct and the negations of tautologies as being incorrect. We do speak of committal attitudes toward propositions as correct or incorrect. But entertainment is not a commital attitude. Entertaining the proposition that o is so-and-so is the attitude that is common to *all forms of occurrently cognizing* o as being so-and-so—including *imagining* o to be so-and-so, *wondering whether* o is so-and-so, *visualizing* o as so-and-so, and *conceiving* of o as being so-and-so. Many of these don't have correctness conditions that depend on o's being so-and-so. We don't say that it is *incorrect* to imagine o as being so-and-so, to wonder whether o is so-and-so, to visualize o as so-and-so, or to conceive of o as being so-and-so simply because o isn't so-and-so. Since entertaining the proposition that o is so-and-so is the attitude that is common to these and other forms of occurrently cognizing o as being so-and-so, it doesn't have correctness conditions that depend on o's being so-and-so, either.

This brings us to Hanks's objection.

> It is crucial for Soames that acts of predication can be true or false. . . . In addition, he regards acts of predication as neutral, in the sense that in predicating a property of an object, the subject takes no position about whether the object has the property. Now, consider what we might call a *pure* act of predicating the property of being F of an object a, this is a simple, stand-alone, ordinary act of predication. . . . [F]or Soames, a pure act of predicating F of a is not a judgment that a is F, since judgment requires an additional act of endorsing one's act of predication.[1]

There is nothing clearly wrong here, but there is a potential problem in the wings. In speaking of a *pure, stand-alone act of predication* that one endorses in making a judgment, Hanks may be thinking of judgment as a cognitive operation that takes the pure act of predication as input and produces an output which, *because it is committal*, has both truth and correctness conditions. That isn't my picture. Hanks continues.

---

[1] Hanks 2014, 15–16.

Now suppose that a is not F. If so, then this act of predication is false, and hence the agent did something incorrect. The agent made a mistake. But how could the agent have made a mistake, if she took no stand one way or the other about whether a is F? It is incoherent to suppose an agent can make a mistake by predicating F of a while taking no position at all about whether a is F.[2]

Hanks thinks that the agent has made a mistake, because he thinks that truth and correctness conditions are one and the same.

I am relying on the fact that acts of predication have correctness conditions, in the form of truth conditions. An act of predicating F of a is *correct, that is, true*, iff a is F.[3]

But are truth and correctness one and the same?

In some cases, they seem to be. Consider committal acts, dispositions, or states, like *judging, believing, assuming*, or *predicting*. Corresponding to these are nominal forms—*judgments, beliefs*, and *assumptions*, which are, pretty much, said to be correct iff true, and predictions, which are said to be correct iff they *come true*. Contrasting with these are various noncommittal acts, dispositions, or states—e.g., *hoping, wishing*, and *praying*. One who hopes, wishes, or prays for the sun to shine tomorrow is not committed to the sun's really shining tomorrow. Consequently, we don't think of such hopes, wishes, or prayers as being *correct* in the way that, say, judgments are. Nor, it may be observed, do we speak of one's hopes, wishes, or prayers, as being true. Nevertheless, we do think of truth as being in the offing. We speak of one's wishes or prayers *coming true*, despite the fact that wishing or praying that the sun will shine

[2] Ibid., 16.
[3] Ibid.

tomorrow doesn't commit one to the sun's shining tomorrow. In these cases, we seem to have assessments of truth without corresponding assessments of correctness.

The reason that entertaining the proposition that o is so-and-so may be true despite being forceless is that, being identical with the proposition that o is so-and-so, it is the common element uniting all manner of committal and noncommittal attitudes. Attitudes such as judgment, belief, knowledge, and assertion are all committal, in the sense that they are correct iff what one judges, believes, knows, or asserts is true. By contrast, attitudes such as doubt, desire, wish, and hope are noncommittal, and so lacking in correctness conditions. Nevertheless, what one doubts, wishes, hopes, or desires—e.g., that the sun will shine tomorrow—may be true. If asked *What did you doubt?* I may answer *That arithmetic is incomplete, which turned out to be true.* If asked *What did you desire yesterday?* I may answer *Yesterday, I desired that the sun would shine today, which, I am happy to say, has turned out to be true.* We can even do something like this for *wish* and *hope.* If asked *What did you wish and hope for yesterday?* I may answer *What I wished and hoped for yesterday was that the sun would shine today, which, even then, was determined to be true by the high-pressure system just off the coast.*

The point to remember is that attitude verbs come in all varieties—from positively committal, like 'judge' and 'believe', to epistemically noncommittal, like 'wish', 'desire', 'hope', 'imagine', and 'fantasize', to negatively committal, like 'deny' and 'dispute'. In all these cases, we can speak of *what I have judged, believed, wished, desired, hoped, imagined, fantasized, denied, disputed,* which may, in turn, be evaluated for truth. To me, this suggests that it is not any of these particular attitudes but their objects that, in the first instance, represent things as being certain ways, and so have truth conditions independently of agents' further affirmative, negative, or noncommittal stances toward them. This is captured by abstracting the attitude of entertaining as an act that is performed in various ways by agents who bear any of the more specialized attitudes, in something like the way in which traveling from point A to point B is something one does when one walks, jogs, runs, crawls, or in general moves from A to B. This act of entertaining, which is the proposition entertained, has truth conditions because it represents things as being certain ways. It doesn't have correctness conditions because, being the core component of all the attitudes, it must be noncommittal.

Worries, Opportunities, and Unsolved Problems

In this final chapter I will discuss some currently unanswered questions that arise for the framework I have proposed when one both expands its scope and presses for more detailed treatment of some of the matters heretofore sketched only in general terms. The first worry is why, if propositions are the common objects of so-called *propositional attitudes*, the verbs in (1a) and (1b) differ in the complements they take.

1a. believe, assert, confirm, affirm, assume, posit
1b. think, say, claim, judge, conjecture, suppose

Whereas the former take both *that*-clauses and noun phrases of the form *the proposition that S* as arguments, the latter take only *that*-clauses, plus expressions like 'something', as in (2),

2a. John thought/said/claimed *something that Mary also thought/ said/claimed.*
2b. Mary supposed *something sensible*, whereas John supposed *something absurd.*

or 'what so-and-so v-ed', as in (3).

3a. Susan said *what Joe merely thought.*
3b. Sam boldly claimed *what Mary merely supposed* and Joe *cautiously conjectured.*

Although the details of these constructions are daunting, I doubt the differences between them undermines the significance of propositions in their semantic analyses.[1]

With this in mind, consider the pairs in (4–9).

4a. Joe *thinks* that the Earth is round.

4b. Joe *believes* that the Earth is round.

5a. Joe *said* that the Earth is round.

5b. Joe *asserted* that the Earth is round.

6a. Joe *claimed* that the Earth is round.

6b. Joe *confirmed* that the Earth is round.

7a. Joe *judged* that the Earth is round.

7b. Joe *affirmed* that the Earth is round.

8a. Joe *conjectured* that the Earth is round.

8b. Joe *assumed* that the Earth is round

9a. Joe *supposed* that the Earth was round.

9b. Joe *posited* that the Earth is round.

Despite the syntactic differences between the two classes of verbs, it is hard to see any significant difference in the propositions expressed by (4a) and (4b). There are some minor differences in the other (a)–(b) pairs, but it is far from clear that these differences involve propositional versus nonpropositional objects.

What might these verbal differences amount to? Suppose we take 'believe', 'assert', 'confirm', 'affirm', 'assume', and 'posit' to be two-place predicates of agents and propositions, which are provided by the *extensions* of their subject and object expressions. By contrast, suppose we take 'think', 'say', 'claim', 'judge', 'conjecture', and 'suppose' to be operators that designate functions mapping the *semantic*

[1] Although all the verbs in (1) can take *that*-clauses, there are differences in the ease with which some of the verbs in (ii) take quantifiers and *wh*-clauses. 'Judge', for example, seems to resist them.

contents of—i.e., propositions expressed by—their sentential arguments onto one-place predicates of their subjects. On this analysis, the proposition *that Joe believes that the Earth is round* is identical with the proposition *that Joe thinks that the Earth is round*, even though the routes from the two attitude-reporting sentences to the proposition they both express are different. Since 'believe' looks for the extensions of its arguments, we combine 'that' with the sentence S that follows it to form a directly referential singular term the extension of which is the semantic content of S. This gives us the propositional argument of the two-place predicate. Since *think* looks not for the extension of its sentential argument, but for its semantic content, we map that content directly onto the one-place property of believing the proposition expressed by S, *without going through the intermediate step of assigning it as the extension of any term.*

On this analysis, 'think' cannot, but 'believe' can, take arguments like 'the proposition that Susan denied', (in part) because the semantic content of that argument isn't the sort of thing that can be true or false, whereas its extension can. Similar remarks could be made about 'say' vs. 'assert', 'claim' vs. 'confirm', 'judge' vs. 'affirm', 'conjecture' vs. 'assume', and 'suppose' vs. 'posit' pairs. On this picture, the analysis of attitude ascriptions involving verbs in (1a) follows roughly a Fregean pattern, while the analysis of attitude ascriptions involving verbs in (1b) follows roughly a Carnapian pattern (characterized in chapter 1 of *Meaning and Necessity* as the "method of intension and extension"). Although this incipient analysis is only a suggested beginning, it is not, I think, an impossible stretch.[2] In sum,

---

[2] We might expand the analysis by taking 'what Bill denied' to be a higher-order quantifier that moves from post-verbal position to the front, leaving an objectual variable ranging over propositions in its place in logical form. Clausal variables of this sort are treated by (1a) and (1b) verbs as clauses generally are—i.e., as singular terms denoting their propositional extensions (relative to assignments) by (1a) verbs, and as sentences expressing propositional semantic contents (relative to as-

the mere existence of different argument types for different classes of verbs doesn't show that sentences containing them don't report genuine *propositional* attitudes.

Next, I turn to an issue that arises for defenders of semantic versions of Millianism about proper names and natural kind terms. The issue concerns so-called "empty names," which don't refer to anything. Do such terms prevent us from combining semantic Millianism with the cognitive conception of propositions? In addressing this question, I set aside names like 'Socrates' that have referents that no longer exist, as well as names like 'Lilly Pad', which refers to the doghouse I plan to construct for my dog Lilly from an elaborate set of plans I have drawn up, using already purchased building materials. I further set aside the name 'Lilly Polyana' that designates a certain lavish doghouse I previously planned to build, and could still build, but never will. I also skip names like 'Hamlet' that refer to fictional characters, which are abstract artifacts.

I don't put aside names like 'Vulcan' and 'phlogiston' that, on some accounts, fail to refer to anything. Suppose, for the sake of argument, that these are genuine names that occur in the true sentences (10a) and (10b).

10a. Vulcan doesn't exist.
10b. Phlogiston doesn't exist.

How, if the names are empty, do these sentences manage to express truths? One standard account claims that they express *gappy propositions*. If propositions are mysterious *know-not-whats*, or artificial

---

signments) by (1b) verbs. This would explain examples like 'Bill boldly asserted what Mark merely conjectured', despite the fact that 'assert' is a two-place relational predicate, while 'conjecture' doesn't take singular term objects. If asked why we can't be get *Bill boldly asserted logicism but Mark merely conjectured it', the answer is that 'conjecture' can take a sentential complement but not a singular term argument.

models constructed for our theoretical convenience, positing gappy propositions doesn't add much to the already impenetrable mystery of how any propositions can play central roles in our cognitive lives. Nor is there a problem of assigning the right truth values to gappy propositions expressed by non-hyperintensional sentences. The problem for such views is *differentiating* what ought to be the different gappy propositions believed by agents A and B, when A believes that Vulcan doesn't exist but B believes that phlogiston doesn't exist.

The problem for the cognitive conception of propositions is the reverse. Consider the cognitive act *predicating* the property P using name n to identify its predication target*, where *predicating* P using n* is just like *predicating P using n* except that no object need be determined in order for predication* to occur.[3] If, we count this cognitive act as a proposition, then differentiating the proposition *that Vulcan exists* from the proposition *that phlogiston exists* will be straightforward. The former incorporates a Millian mode of presentation involving the name 'Vulcan', while the latter incorporates a Millian mode involving 'phlogiston'. Since neither predicates anything of anything, neither has truth conditions. Since things that don't have truth conditions aren't true, these gappy propositions aren't true. Thus, the proposition *that it is not true that Vulcan exists* is itself true, as is the distinct proposition *that it is not true that phlogiston exists*. From here it is a short step to differentiating the truth believed by one who says "It's not true that Vulcan exists" from the truth believed by one who says "It is not true that phlogiston exists."

All this is easy if we admit acts of *predicating** into the class of propositions. In a way, the step isn't a large one, since we already recognize *predicating planethood of Venus identifying the putative*

---

[3] More precisely, it is just like what I have elsewhere called 'directly predicating (P using n)'.

predication target using the name 'Hesperus'. Although this is *predication** using a name that designates something, it is cognitively indistinguishable from *predication** using a name that merely purports to designate something but doesn't. This suggests it might not be an impossible stretch to expand the class of propositions to include not only *purely representational cognitive acts* but also acts that purport to be such, but fail because one of their sub-acts involves using a representational vehicle (in this case, a name or kind term) that fails to determine a propositional constituent.

But there is still another worry. Let A be an agent who can't predicate properties of propositions, or if she can, hasn't mastered the concept of truth. It may be unrealistic to suppose that A can predicate* existence using the name 'Vulcan', and so entertain the proposition *that Vulcan exists*, but it isn't obviously incoherent to suppose she can. Still, even if A can entertain this proposition, A can't negate it. The negation operation discussed in chapter 2 operates on a proposition that represents something x as being F to yield a proposition that represents arbitrary objects as *not being such that x is F*. Since, with Vulcan, no x is represented, the negation operation is undefined for the proposition *that Vulcan exists*. Without some plausible work-around—which I don't see—this means (i) that agents that lack the concept of truth can't do truth-functional cognition with propositions that incorporate empty names as Millian modes of presentation, and (ii) that truth-functional cognition of sophisticated agents involving such propositions must be construed as invoking a truth predicate. Perhaps these results aren't disqualifying, but they are unsolved problems, *if it turns out that semantics really does require Millian names that are genuinely empty.*

My final worry involves extending the cognitive account of the semantic contents of declarative sentences to include cognitive contents of interrogative and imperative sentences. I close with three provisional ideas. The first concerns yes/no questions like the one that is the object of the attitude reported by a use of (11).

11. John asked whether snow is white.

Whereas the proposition *that snow is white* represents the world as being a certain way, and so has truth conditions, it is natural to suppose that the question *whether snow is white* is not the sort of thing that is true or false. However, it should be closely related to the proposition. After all, we don't want the compositional semantics of questions to be disconnected from the semantics of corresponding declaratives.

With this in mind, suppose we take the question to be the act of cognizing the property *being such that snow is white* by applying the operation that generates *being such that so-and-so* from the proposition *that so-and-so*, which one identifies by entertaining it. To *ask* this question is to request an answer—where 'yes' represents something (indeed everything) as having the property and 'no' represents each thing as not having it. On this picture, answers to yes/no questions have truth conditions, but the questions themselves don't.

How might we think about the *wh*-question Q illustrated in (12)?

12. John asked which Fs are Gs.

Perhaps it is the act of cognizing the property *being all the Fs of which some are Gs* by applying an operation that generates it from the proposition *that some Fs are Gs*, which one identifies by entertaining it. On this picture, to *ask* Q is to request a complete specification of those Fs. Since Q doesn't represent anything as being any way, it doesn't have truth conditions. But one who understands what it is to ask Q knows that one who answers Q by saying *that Bob and Ted are G* presupposes that Bob and Ted are F, asserts they are Gs, and implicates that one knows of no other relevant F who is G.

Finally, consider the imperative sentence (13).

13. Close the door.

What is the semantic content of this sentence relative to a context, and what is required to understand it? Regarding the first question, the two key elements appear to be the individual, or individuals, being addressed in the context and the act *closing the door* expressed by the verb phrase. Regarding the second question, two things appear to be needed: (i) the ability to use the sentence with its semantic content, (ii) knowledge of the speech acts—advisings, requests, instructions, orders, commands, and the like—standardly performed by uses of it. Taking a directive to be that which is common to all these speech acts, we may identify the directive expressed by a use of (13) in a context in which I am the one who is addressed to be the univocal content of the 'that' clause that appears in my uses of the sentences in (14).[4]

14a. The boss's advice was that I close the door.
14b. The boss's request was that I close the door.
14c. The boss's instruction was that I close the door.
14d. The boss's order was that I close the door.
14e. The boss's command was that I close the door.

What is the common content? Perhaps it is the act of cognizing the pair consisting of me and the act of closing the door by applying an operation that generates it from the proposition *that SS closes the door*, identified by entertaining it. To take this act, the directive, to have been suggested, requested, instructed, ordered, or commanded by the boss is to take the boss to have advised, requested, instructed, ordered, or commanded me (the first member of the cognized pair) to perform the act that is the second member of the pair. On this

---

[4] I borrow the term 'directive' from my student Matt Babb, whose research on imperatives has influenced my thinking on this subject. That said, it should not be assumed that he endorses the preliminary remarks I make here.

picture, the directive itself doesn't have truth conditions because it doesn't represent anything as being any way. But there is a common element in the truth conditions of my use of the sentences in (15).

15a. The boss advised that I close the door.
15b. The boss requested that I close the door.
15c. The boss instruction that I close the door.
15d. The boss ordered that I close the door.
15e. The boss commanded that I close the door.

The common element is that the boss directed me to perform an action that results in the door being closed. The common element in the truth conditions of my use of the sentences in (16) is the proposition *that I closed the door,* which, of course, represents the world as being a certain way.

16a. I followed the boss's advice/instruction/order/command that I close the door.
16b. I complied with the boss's request that I close the door.

These final issues, involving questions and imperatives, are among the most important currently unsolved problems for the cognitive conception of propositions. While the ideas about them just presented are preliminary, and not intended to be definitive, they are prompted by what I hope is an understandable conviction. If propositions—which are the contents of cognitions and speech acts associated with uses of most declarative sentences—are cognitive acts of the kind I have identified, then surely the contents of cognitions and speech acts associated with uses of interrogative and imperative sentences must be cognitive acts that are reasonably related to those that have made up most of the subject matter of this book. Identifying these acts and integrating them into the cognitive conception is a high priority.

REFERENCES

❖

Bowman, Brian. 2012. *Linguistic Understanding and Semantic Theory*. Unpublished dissertation. University of Southern California.

Burgess, John. 1996. "Marcus, Kripke, and Names." *Philosophical Studies* 84:1–47.

Carnap, Rudolf. 1947. *Meaning and Necessity*. Chicago: Chicago University Press; second, expanded edition, 1956.

Cartwright, Richard. 1962. "Propositions." In R. J. Butler, ed., *Analytic Philosophy*, First Series. Oxford: Blackwell, 81–103; reprinted in Richard Cartwright, *Philosophical Essays*, Cambridge, MA: MIT Press, 1987, 33–53.

Castaneda, H. 1966. "'He': A Study in the Logic of Self-Consciousness." *Ratio* 8:130–57.

———. 1967. "Indicators and Quasi-Indicators." *American Philosophical Quarterly* 4:85–100.

———. 1968. "On the Logic of Attributions of Self-Knowledge to Others." *Journal of Philosophy* 65:439–56.

Chalmers, David. 1996. *The Conscious Mind*. New York and Oxford: Oxford University Press.

———. 2002. "The Components of Content." In David Chalmers, ed., *Philosophy of Mind: Classical and Contemporary Readings*, Oxford: Oxford University Press, 608–33.

———. 2011. "Propositions and Propositional Attitude Ascriptions: A Fregean Account," *Noûs* 45:595–639.

Church, Alonzo. 1988. "A Remark Concerning Quine's Paradox about Modality." In Nathan Salmon and Scott Soames, eds., *Propositions and Attitudes*, Oxford: Oxford University Press, 58–65.

Davidson, Donald. 2001. "Truth and Meaning." *Inquiries into Truth and Interpretation*, Oxford: Clarendon Press, 2001, 17–36. Originally published in *Synthese* 17 (1967):304–23.

Fine, Kit. 2007. *Semantic Relationism*, Malden MA: Blackwell.

Frege, Gottlob. 1997. *The Frege Reader*. Ed. and trans. Michael Beaney. Oxford Blackwell.

Dickie, Imogen. 2010. "We Are Acquainted with Ordinary Things." In Jeshion (2010a), 213–45.

Hanks, Peter. 2014. "Three Pictures of Propositional Content." Paper delivered at the Central APA Symposium on Naturalistic Theories of Propositions, Chicago, February 26.

Hawthorne, John, and Manley, David. 2012. *The Reference Book*. New York: Oxford University Press.

Jackson, Frank. 1982. "Epiphenomenal Qualia." *Philosophical Quarterly* 32:127–36.

———. 1986. "What Mary Didn't Know." *Journal of Philosophy* 83:191–95.

———. 1998a. *From Metaphysics to Ethics*. Oxford: Clarendon Press.

———. 1998b. "Reference and Description Revisited." *Philosophical Perspectives* 12:201–18.

———. 2007. "Reference and Description from the Descriptivist's Corner." *Philosophical Books* 48:17–26.

Jeshion, Robin. 2002. "Acquaintanceless *De Re* Belief." In J. Campbell, M. O. O'Rourke, and D. Shier, eds., *Meaning and Truth: Investigations in Philosophical Semantics*, New York: Seven Bridges Press, 53–78.

——— (ed.). 2010a. *New Essays on Singular Thought*. Oxford: Oxford University Press.

———. 2010b. "Singular Thought: Acquaintance, Semantic Instrumentalism, and Cognitivism." In Jeshion (2010a), 105–40.

Kaplan, David. 1979. "On the Logic of Demonstratives." *Journal of Philosophical Logic* 8:81–98.

———. 1989. "Demonstratives: An Essay on the Semantics, Logic, Metaphysics and Epistemology of Demonstratives and Other Indexicals." In Joseph Almog, John Perry, and Howard Wettstein, eds., *Themes from Kaplan*, New York: Oxford University Press, 481–563.

King, Jeffrey, Scott Soames, and Jeffrey Speaks. 2014. *New Thinking about Propositions*. Oxford: Oxford University Press.

Kripke, Saul. 1972. "Naming and Necessity." in Donald Davidson and Gilbert Harman, eds., *Semantics of Natural Languages*, Dordrecht: Reidel, 253–355. Reissued as *Naming and Necessity*, Cambridge: Harvard University Press, 1980.

———.1979. "A Puzzle about Belief." In Avishi Margalit, ed., *Meaning and Use*, Dordrecht: Reidel, 239–83; reprinted in Peter Ludlow, ed., *Readings in the Philosophy of Language*, Cambridge: MIT Press, 1997, 875–920.

———. 2008. "Frege's Theory of Sense and Reference." *Theoria* 74:181–218.

———. 2011a. "The First Person." In *Philosophical Troubles*, Oxford: Oxford University Press, 292–321.

———. 2011b. "Unrestricted Exportation and Some Morals for the Philosophy of Language." In *Philosophical Troubles*, Oxford: Oxford University Press, 322–50.

Lewis, David. 1979. "Attitudes *De Dicto* and *De Se*." *Philosophical Review* 88:513–43; reprinted in *Philosophical Papers*, vol. 1, New York: Oxford University Press, 133–55.

Nagel, Thomas. 1974. "What Is It Like to Be a Bat?" *Philosophical Review* 83:435–50.

Perry, John. 1977. "Frege on Demonstratives." *Philosophical Review* 86:474–97.

———. 1979. "The Essential Indexical." *Noûs* 13:3–21.

———. 2001a. *Knowledge, Possibility, and Consciousness*. Cambridge, MA. MIT Press.

———. 2001b. *Reference and Reflexivity*. Stanford, CA: Center for the Study of Language and Information.

Putnam, Hilary. 1970. "Is Semantics Possible?" *Metaphilosophy* 1:187–201; reprinted in Hilary Putnam, *Philosophical Papers*, vol. 2, Cambridge: Cambridge University Press, 1975, 139–52.

———. 1973. "Explanation and Reference." In G. Pearce and P. Maynard, eds., *Conceptual Change*, Dordrecht: Reidel, 199–221; reprinted in Putnam, *Philosophical Papers*, vol. 2, 196–214.

———. 1975. "The Meaning of 'Meaning.'" In K. Gunderson, ed., *Language, Mind, and Knowledge*, Minnesota Studies in the Philosophy of Science, 7, Minneapolis: University of Minnesota Press, 131–93; reprinted in Putnam, *Philosophical Papers*, vol. 2, 215–71.

Recanati, François. 2010. "Singular Thought: In Defense of Acquaintance." In Jeshion (2010a), 141–89.

Reiber, Stephen. 1992. "Understanding Synonyms without Knowing That They Are Synonymous." *Analysis* 52:224–28.

Richard, Mark. 1993. "Articulated Terms." *Philosophical Perspectives* 7:207–30.

Russell, Bertrand. 1905. "On Denoting." *Mind* 14:479–93.

Salmon, Nathan. 1986. *Frege's Puzzle*. Cambridge MA: MIT Press.

———. 1987. "Existence." In James Tomberlin, ed., *Philosophical Perspectives* 1:49–108.

———. 1989a. "How to Become a Millian Heir." *Noûs* 23:211–20.

———. 1989b. "Tense and Singular Propositions." In Joseph Almog, John Perry, and Howard Wettstein, eds., *Themes from Kaplan*, New York: Oxford University Press, 331–92.

———. 1990. "A Millian Heir Rejects the Wages of *Sinn*." in C. A. Anderson and J. Owens, eds., *Propositional Attitudes: The Role of Content in Logic, Language, and Mind*, Stanford CA: CSLI, 215–47.

———. 2002. "Demonstrating and Necessity." *Philosophical Review* 111:497–537.

———. 2005. "On Designating." *Mind* 114:1069–1133.

———. 2010. "Three Perspectives on *Quantifying In*." In Jeshion (2010a), 64–76.

———. 2012. "Recurrence." *Philosophical Studies* 159:407–41.

Soames, Scott. 1987. "Direct Reference, Propositional Attitudes, and Semantic Content." *Philosophical Topics* 14:47–87; reprinted in Soames 2009c, 33–71.

———. 2002. *Beyond Rigidity*. New York: Oxford University Press.

———. 2003. *Philosophical Analysis in the Twentieth Century*, vol. 2. Princeton and Oxford: Princeton University Press.

———. 2005a. "*Beyond Rigidity*: Reply to McKinsey." *Canadian Journal of Philosophy* 35:169–78.

———. 2005b. "Naming and Asserting." In Zoltan Szabo, ed., *Semantics vs. Pragmatics*, New York and Oxford: Oxford University Press, 356–52; reprinted in Soames 2009a, 251–77.

———. 2005c. *Reference and Description*. Princeton and Oxford: Princeton University Press.

———. 2006a. "The Philosophical Significance of the Kripkean Necessary Aposteriori." *Philosophical Issues* 16:288–309.

———. 2006b. "Reply to Critics of Beyond Rigidity." *Philosophical Studies* 128:711–38.

———. 2006c. "Understanding Assertion." In Judith Thomson and Alex Byrne, eds., *Content and Modality*. Oxford. Oxford University Press; reprinted in Soames 2009c, 211–42.

———. 2007a. "Actually." In Mark Kalderon, ed., *Proceedings of the Aristotelian Society*, supplementary volume 81:251–77, reprinted in Soames 2009c, 277–99.

———. 2007b. "The Substance and Significance of the Dispute over Two Dimensionalism." *Philosophical Books* 48:34–49.

———. 2007c. "What Are Natural Kinds?" *Philosophical Topics* 35:329–42; reprinted in Soames 2014a, 265–80.

———. 2008. "Why Propositions Cannot be Sets of Truth-Supporting Circumstances." *Journal of Philosophical Logic* 37:267–76; reprinted in Soames 2009c, 72–80.

———. 2009a. "The Gap between Meaning and Assertion: Why What We Literally Say Often Differs from What Our Words Literally Mean." In Soames 2009b, 278–97.

———. 2009b. *Philosophical Essays*, vol. 1. Princeton, NJ: Princeton University Press.

———. 2009c. *Philosophical Essays*, vol. 2. Princeton, NJ: Princeton University Press.

———. 2010a. *Philosophy of Language*. Princeton, NJ: Princeton University Press.

———. 2010b. "True At." *Analysis* 71:124–33.

———. 2010c. *What Is Meaning?* Princeton, NJ: Princeton University Press.

———. 2011. "Kripke on Epistemic and Metaphysical Possibility." In Alan Berger, ed., *Saul Kripke*, Cambridge: Cambridge University Press, 2011, 78–99; reprinted in Soames 2014a, 167–88.

———. 2012. "Two Versions of Millianism." In Joseph Campbell, Michael O'Rourke, and Harry Silverstein, eds., *Reference and Referring, Topics in Philosophy, Vol. 10* (Cambridge: MIT Press), 83–118; reprinted in Soames 2014a, 231–64.

———. 2014a. *Analytic Philosophy in America and Other Historical and Contemporary Essays*. Princeton, NJ: Princeton University Press.

———. 2014b. *The Analytic Tradition in Philosophy*, vol. 1. Princeton, NJ: Princeton University Press.

———. 2014c. "The Place of Quine in Analytic Philosophy." In Gilbert Harman and Ernest Lepore, eds., *Companion to W.V.O. Quine*. Malden, MA: Wiley Blackwell; reprinted in Soames 2014a, 104–38.

———. 2014d. "Why the Possible-Worlds Conception of Propositions Can't Be Correct," "Propositions as Cognitive Event Types," and "Clarifying and Improving the Cognitive Theory," chapters 3, 6, and 12 of King, Soames, and Speaks 2014.

Thau, Michael. 2002. *Consciousness and Cognition*. Oxford: Oxford University Press.

INDEX

❖